THE TEENAGE GUIDE TO DIGITAL WELLBEING

Collins

Published by Collins
An imprint of HarperCollins Publishers
Westerhill Road, Bishopbriggs,
Glasgow G64 2QT

www.harpercollins.co.uk

HarperCollins Publishers
Macken House, 39/40 Mayor Street Upper,
Dublin 1, D01 C9W8 Ireland

© HarperCollins Publishers 2024

Collins © is a registered trademark
of HarperCollins Publishers Ltd.

Text © 2024 Tanya Goodin

Illustration: Rae Goddard
Publisher: Beth Ralston
Project Leader: Gillian Bowman
Design: Kevin Robbins and James Hunter
Production: Ilaria Rovera

For Ellie and Finn, the inspiration for everything.

978-0-00-865998-1

Printed in India by Replika Press Pvt. Ltd.

10 9 8 7 6 5 4 3 2 1

THE TEENAGE GUIDE TO DIGITAL WELLBEING

FIND THE BALANCE TO LIVE YOUR BEST LIFE

BY DIGITAL WELLBEING EXPERT
TANYA GOODIN

Contents

So, what's digital wellbeing all about?

Digital wellbeing is about striking the right balance between your online and offline life, making sure that the time you spend on screens enhances your health and happiness and doesn't overshadow the uniquely real-world experiences that make life meaningful. You can think of it as being mindful of your digital consumption (what you do on screens) to stay mentally and emotionally healthy and happy.

It's important to be mindful of your digital use because of the particular way the digital world is designed. It's an incredible place; entertainment, education, connection with friends – all at your fingertips. But so much of the internet is one big advertising machine. It's deliberately designed to keep us online for as long as possible, with the hope of selling something to us as we scroll.

That makes it very hard for everyone, adults and teens alike, to log off, put their screens down and go and do something else.

And even when we're very happily online, some of the features designed to keep us there for longer can make some of the internet a not-very-nice place.

It's no wonder that:

o 56% of teens say they wish social media had never been invented

o 60% of adults* say they are 'hooked' on their devices. (* you probably know one that is!)

So, how do you live your best life both online and off? And how do you use your smartphone and the digital world for all the good stuff, but not the bad?

That's what digital wellbeing, and this book, is all about! It's your route map to living healthily and happily with your smartphone and other devices. It will help you work out how to make sure that all your online activities keep you happy and healthy, and also how to find time for some of the experiences and joys that only life offline can bring. The sweet spot of the balance between the two is what we call achieving digital wellbeing.

You're going to go on a journey of discovery to find your very own state of digital wellbeing. This book will be your guide.

Creating a logbook

To make the most of your journey towards discovering digital wellbeing, try creating a logbook of your journey as you work through this book. Logbooks were originally developed by sailors many years ago to help them keep track of wind speeds, direction, distances and positions on their nautical voyages.

Looking back at old logbooks we can see they are very visual records of each journey at sea, with a huge variety of unique symbols, scribbles and notes added by the person keeping the log. They're quite different from journals in that they're not just words, they use pictures and shapes and diagrams to build up a vivid picture of a journey.

Keeping a logbook of your journey to digital wellbeing will help you notice and create healthy habits around your life online, and off. The knowledge you gain about yourself from filling in and viewing your logbook will make you mindful of your digital habits. And being mindful of your digital habits is the key to digital wellbeing.

To start keeping a logbook you will need:

- o   This book (there's a section at the end of every chapter for your 'log')
- o   Coloured pens and pencils
- o   Your own 'visual key' of what you are logging.

Your visual key

Your logbook's visual key will be your way of recording the things you are doing that are helping you achieve your goals (see Month 1). To spark some ideas, the examples on the right represent time with friends, time spent off screens, time spent outside, and time spent trying out a new analogue activity (in this case, chess), amongst others. These are the kinds of things you'll be logging throughout the book.

But you should also think about what *you* want to log that aligns with your unique goals and design a visual key that fits with that. You really don't have to be remotely artistic to design a visual key of symbols that work for you – anything simple that you attach your own meaning to is ideal.

= time with friends offline

= time in nature

= chess

= 1–hour screen break

= tacos!

= time I felt <u>really</u> happy

= meditation

= time I faced a challenge head–on

Your logbook is entirely personal to you; the symbols and tracking around your digital wellbeing don't need to make sense to anyone else. It's your own unique code – it can be as easy or as complicated to understand as you want it to be.

Sample logbook

Here's an idea of what a completed logbook for one month might look like. This person has been logging lots of different hobbies and habits – from the number of times they meditated or practised their art, to how many times they enjoyed their favourite food, tacos! You can refer back to this example for inspiration as you progress with your own logbook.

crafting

1-hour screen breaks

tacos!

times I felt <u>really</u> happy

went to football

meditation

acts of self-care

 went for walks
without my phone

 hung out with
friends offline

 played chess (and won twice!)

 faced a challenge head-on

 times I displayed a strength
(practised my art)

 tried a new analogue
activity ... jigsaws!

Start Mindfully
Month 1

Your habits become your values.

Mahatma Gandhi

Setting your goals

Who do you want to be?

What sort of person do you want to be? What do you want to do with your life? How do you want to earn a living? What are your values and beliefs? How do you want your friends to think about you, and to describe you?

These may not be questions that you've given very much thought to yet in your life, but now is a really good time to start.

The relationship between goals and habits

So much of the person we become as we grow older is grounded in the habits we develop when we are young. This month, I want to encourage you to think about setting some goals for your life (or even for just the next year), and then think about how to identify and develop the healthy habits you will need to help you achieve those goals. But first, let's think a bit about goal setting. For this you're going to need to write your goals down.

The power of writing down goals

We seem to be able to conclude, from looking at lots of research on goal setting, that those who write their goals down have a much better chance of achieving them than those who don't.

In 2007, a group of researchers at Dominican University studied the effectiveness of writing down goals using people recruited from a wide range of different businesses and industries. They divided the people into three groups and asked one group to just think about their goals, another to write down their goals, and the third to write down their goals with their commitments to the action they would take to achieve them, and to share them with others. The group who wrote down their goals and shared them with others were significantly more successful in achieving them, while both of the groups who wrote down their goals were altogether about 50% more successful than the one group who didn't.

Your goals are personal to you. They could be to do with your life at school, your interests, your friendships, places you want to visit – anything really. Here are some examples of goals:

My goals (for now):

I want to be better at tennis!

I want to read more.

I want to spend more time with my friends.

Make your goals S M A R T

As well as writing down your goals, it can be useful and motivating to think about how to make them **S M A R T**.

That is, they should be:

Specific – Make sure your goal is well defined and be clear about what you want to achieve.

Measurable – Consider how you will measure your progress. What small steps do you need to take to reach your goal?

Achievable – Be realistic about what you can manage, and don't overwhelm yourself by trying to do everything at once.

Relevant – Ask yourself whether this goal is going to help you accomplish your wider objectives and get you to where you want to be.

Timed – Set yourself a deadline , which will help you to stay motivated and keep you accountable.

So, consider goals such as *'I will run 100 metres in 15 seconds by Sports Day'* rather than *'I want to run faster'*, or *'I will audition for the school play this term'* rather than *'I want to take part in more activities outside the classroom'*, or *'I will spend no more than 20 minutes scrolling social media in the evening'* rather than *'I want to spend less time on social media.'*

Take some time to write down three **S M A R T** goals here:

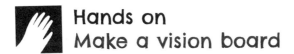

1

2

3

Once you've thought a bit about your goals, we can move on to the habits you will need to help you achieve those goals.

Hands on
Make a vision board

Do this with a friend. Each of you should collect and cut out images, words, pictures of objects, patterns and designs, etc. that represent your goals in life. Choose from as wide a range of sources as possible (magazines, newspapers, websites, fabrics, prints of photos you've taken yourself, etc.). Grab some glue sticks and arrange your selection of words, pictures and fabrics on a piece of paper. Discuss with each other what your personal vision board means to you.

Healthy habits

What do healthy habits look like?

A habit is something you do over and over again, and a healthy daily habit can help you achieve your goals quicker. This can be exercising daily to maintain good physical and mental health, or learning a new word in a foreign language every day if your goal is to become fluent. They are deliberate decisions you make every day to make your dreams possible.

A closer look
Dealing with distractions

No one sets out to develop unhealthy habits. But why is it so hard to develop healthy habits and to stick to them?
Why do we get so easily distracted from pursuing our goals?
For many of us, one culprit may increasingly be the role of so-called 'persuasive technology' in our lives.

Tech companies constantly compete for our attention through the various apps and software that we use on our phones and our digital devices. They do this by developing tricks and techniques built into those software and apps that 'persuade' (i.e. manipulate) us to keep us scrolling on our phones and tablets for far longer than we intend to.

A good example of this is the 'auto play next' feature that you will see on streaming services and video platforms. You may have logged on just to watch one episode or video, but when the next one starts to play automatically you are tempted to keep watching for longer.

Tech companies want us to stay on our screens for longer and longer periods of time. Whenever you've found yourself going down a rabbit hole of content online, it's because persuasive technology has taken you there, to prolong your time on screens. It's not because you're lazy or lack self-control. It's because tech is explicitly designed that way.

When you are next online can you spot any trick or feature that might have been deliberately placed there to try and keep you there for longer?

Think about some healthy habits you might want to build or improve on this year and why they are important to you. Consider which ones might help you achieve your goals. Now think about any *unhealthy* habits you would like to eliminate. Is there anything you would like to spend less time doing? Perhaps you can identify something you are currently spending time on that either isn't helping you achieve your goals or isn't keeping you happy or healthy.

Logbook prompt

What are three habits you want to improve or change this year? Why are they important to you? Create a symbol for each of them to add to your logbook at the end of this month.

Game
Habit bingo

Create a bingo board with different habits or activities (for example, 'Read a book', 'Practise gratitude', 'Unplug for an hour', 'Practise shots on goal for football'). Each day, try to complete a line or pattern on the bingo board by engaging in the listed habits. Encourage a friend to try this with you too. Reflect on your experiences at the end of the month.

Revisiting your goals

Take a minute to look back at the goals you have set, or the vision board you have created, and then look at the healthy habits you have decided to log. Can you see a clear relationship between your healthy habits and your goals? Are these the right habits? Are these the things that will make a difference?

You may not know the answer immediately. There will probably be a good deal of experimenting over the next few weeks and months to see what works, but the most important thing to do is to think about the healthy habits you want to build and how they will contribute towards achieving your goals. The steps you've taken so far mean you're in a great place to start.

 ### Offline heroes

Tashi and Nungshi Malik, aka 'The Everest Twins', are mountaineers from India. They were the first female siblings to climb Mount Everest, at just 21. They set themselves a goal to prepare for something they had never experienced before, and couldn't even see: the summit of Everest. It took them three years to persuade their mum to even let them try to do it. Each week they prepared themselves with their own version of healthy habits – a series of endurance, aerobic and strength exercises – as well as focusing on their nutrition. 'Climbing Everest symbolised our ability to dream big and to achieve it by combining passion with commitment,' says Tashi.

....

The power of mindfulness

You have seen how healthy habits can be deliberate, conscious efforts to do something that helps you achieve your goals. And you have seen how persuasive tech can distract us from our goals. So now is a good time to think a bit about the practice of mindfulness and how we can apply that to tech, and to all our other habits.

Mindfulness is the ability to be fully present, conscious and aware of what we are doing. It's the opposite of the kind of mindless scrolling that often takes place when we are on screens, which can make us feel better in the moment, but not so good later on, when we haven't achieved what we wanted to with our time. So, cultivating a habit of mindfulness around screen time is going to be your best weapon against persuasive tech.

The S O S process

Try this three-step process:

 **Stop** – Before you pick up a device, decide what you are doing and how long you will do it for: *'I'm checking my messages, I'll take 20 minutes'*; *'I'm finding out the time of the next bus, I'll take 5 minutes.'*

 **Observe** – Check in with yourself about how you are feeling. Are you tired? Happy? Angry? Purposeful? Bored?

 **Stop (again)** – Check in with yourself again when you put the device down. How long did you end up spending on your task? Did you just do what you intended to do? How do you feel now?

The first few times it might feel as if this process takes a long time. But each time you do this you will find it easier. It's all part of the exercise of training yourself to be more mindful and intentional in your habits.

Mindfulness doesn't have to be just around your time on phones or other devices either. Lots of activities either develop mindfulness or are in themselves mindful – things like yoga, meditation, or mindful walking, for example.

You can use the **S O S** process to increase your mindfulness around any habit that you are trying to lessen or break. Use it to stop and check in with yourself about what your intentions are, and how that habit makes you feel.

 ## Month checklist

1. Create a list, or a vision board, to identify your goals. ☐

2. Reflect on your existing habits and set your intentions for them. ☐

3. Design your logbook. Make it visual in whatever way works for you. ☐

4. Become more aware of your habits with your bingo board. ☐

5. Practise mindfulness around your tech use and other habits, using the **S O S** process. ☐

Month 1 logbook

Start your logbook this month by designing a visual key for your log, like the one on page 9. Remember to include symbols or icons for the three habits you've identified you want to improve or change this year. Include as many other habits as you want and keep track of how often you work on them throughout the month.

Tashi and Nungshi might have
drawn something like this

Love Yourself
Month 2

To love oneself is the beginning of a lifelong romance.

Oscar Wilde

Self-esteem

The importance of liking yourself (a lot)

When we are very young children, we don't tend to worry a lot about our self-esteem (whether we like ourselves). In fact, if asked to stop and think about it, toddlers will probably reply that they like themselves very much indeed! But as we grow older the question of self-esteem can start to become more complicated, and more important, especially as we start to interact with the digital world. Your self-esteem, and how high it is, has been linked to all sorts of things, like your chances of developing mental illness, doing well at school, and the quality of your relationships with other people.

Loving yourself – developing high self-esteem – is an important part of growing up. Thinking about how to develop it, and what things might help or hinder you (online and off!), is what this month is all about.

What does high self-esteem look like?

Self-esteem has been defined in lots of different ways but generally if you have high self-esteem you:

- Have a positive view of yourself
- Are confident, but not arrogant
- Learn from your mistakes rather than being discouraged by them
- Make new friends easily
- Will try and solve problems on your own, but can ask for help when you need to
- Are willing to try new things
- Are proud of your achievements.

What affects your self-esteem?

Lots of very normal life changes can influence your self-esteem: things like changing school, moving house, exams, the birth of a new family member, and even illness, divorce, or money troubles in your family. Self-esteem peaks and troughs at different times throughout your life and that's completely natural. Some events that could impact how you think about yourself may be out of your control, but there are things you can try to avoid which may hurt your self-esteem, and things that you can actively do which will help keep your underlying self-esteem high to better cope with life's challenges.

HELPS
Know your strengths

Understanding your strengths, reminding yourself of them and appreciating them, will help you to build and maintain high self-esteem. It can be tricky to list your own strengths the first time you do it, so it may be easier to think about the qualities you like in your friends and family members. Get together with someone you are close to and ask them to write down three things they really like about you. Do the same for them and then swap your lists.

Do you agree with the other person's thoughts of you? Use that as a starting point to write your own list of strengths if you need to and copy them below. You don't need to stick to three – write as many as you want!

Tip: Your strengths as a person may change as you get older and experience more in life, so use a pencil in this exercise in case you want to make changes to it in the future.

My strengths:
e.g. I am funny and make people laugh.

Offline hero

Shiden Tekle co-founded Legally Black UK with a group of his friends (all aged 17 and 18) after being racially abused from the age of 12 at school. They wanted to draw attention to the lack of positive depictions of the Black community in the media. Together, they re-created film posters for famous films such as *Titanic* and the *Harry Potter* series, replacing all the White faces with the Black faces of their families and friends, who agreed to be photographed to help with their project. Shiden said, 'In big films, Black characters are often playing criminals and drug dealers, and that quickly conditions people to believe that all Black people are like that. So, we decided to put Black faces in the big movies, and challenge people's perceptions and assumptions.' The group made their posters and stuck them in bus stops in their local community in Brixton, London. They soon received nationwide attention for their thought-provoking campaign.

HURTS
Avoid comparing yourself

One thing that can negatively impact your self-esteem is when you compare yourself with other people and decide that their unique strengths are 'better' than yours – something that is all too easy to do when scrolling on social media. This is quite different from admiring and being inspired by another person's achievements and qualities, such as a sporting hero or musician. It's the type of comparison where you feel bad about yourself or put yourself down that you want to avoid. You can see how comparing yourself to another person isn't helpful to do, if you use dogs as an example. Take a labrador and a dachshund. Each breed is quite different, with unique qualities and strengths. Deciding which one is 'best' would find lots of people disagreeing on either side. They're both very different dogs but equally lovable and each has lots of fans. As with people, dogs are very different, but equally as important.

Comparing yourself to other people and losing sight of the wonderful qualities that make you uniquely you is something you should always try to stop yourself doing. You may find yourself doing this more and more if you spend too much time on social media.

Logbook prompt

Design a symbol for your log that represents a time you have recognised or noticed yourself displaying one of your strengths and good qualities. Note in your logbook how many times this month you recognised and appreciated yourself for a strength or quality you displayed.

Social media

An unhealthy habit?

Lots of studies have revealed the negative impact social media can have on our self-esteem. This seems to stem from what's been called the 'comparison culture' created by social media. Seeing a constant stream of curated, retouched and filtered images on our feeds (not just from celebrities but also from our own friends and family) makes it easier to fall into the trap of comparing ourselves to other people and their lives and accomplishments, which is not healthy for our self-esteem.

Comparison is a normal instinct, but social media has turbo-charged the opportunities to do it and amplified its negative effects. When your parents and grandparents were growing up, they could only compare themselves with a limited number of people in their own part of the world (probably just in their neighbourhood), and they likely saw them on both their good and bad days. But you can now compare yourself with billions of people online every day who only tend to show the 'perfect moments' of their lives. And, while your parents could turn off the TV and go to bed, there's no escape now from the temptation to carry on comparing yourself at any time during the day or night thanks to social media being so accessible on different types of technology. (See 'Sleep' on page 37.)

None of the time spent comparing ourselves unfavourably on social media is healthy. Studies have shown that the greater amount of time spent on social media overall, the greater the negative impact on your self-esteem. The particularly sensitive ages seem to be between 11 and 13 for girls and between 14 and 15 for boys, when longer and longer periods of time on social media predict a dip in your life satisfaction a year later. This time of your life is an important one for being with your friends IRL and spending time developing strong and supportive relationships. If you're spending too much time on social media instead, it generally isn't good news for how you feel about yourself.

Hands on
Write a letter to your future self

What advice would you give yourself about the habits you need to maintain your self-esteem as you grow up? Read yours out to a friend and encourage them to do one too.

....

A closer look
'Likes' aren't good for us

The 'like' button is one of the features of persuasive tech that is particularly bad for our self-esteem. Before its invention, people posted pictures on social media for their friends and family to see, with none of the ranking and rating that goes on now thanks to 'likes'. But tech companies wanted to find a way of increasing the amount of time spent on social media platforms and after a lot of experimenting, Facebook was the first to invent a button to 'like' images so people could show their approval, which resulted in more people spending more time and energy on social media.

Interestingly, the software engineer who invented the like button, Justin Rosenstein, has now said that he regrets it. He regards it as something that has significantly contributed to the harm social media can do to peoples' mental health; and studies have backed this. One study found that users' self-esteem dropped in direct proportion to the numbers of likes on each image they viewed.

....

What does healthy use look like?

We do know a bit about what a healthy use of social media may look like:

1. **Connecting with friends** – Using social media in an active way to be genuinely sociable, i.e. messaging friends and strengthening relationships with them, seems to show a positive effect on your wellbeing.

2. **Focusing on you** – Liking and commenting on other people's posts (called 'other-orientated activity' by researchers) has been linked to poorer self-image, whereas posting on your own feed ('self-orientated activity') doesn't have the same negative impact.

3. **Skipping selfies** – Taking and posting selfies has been linked to poor self-esteem, but taking and looking at group pictures of friends, or taking and posting pictures of activities has no negative effect.

4. **Puppies!** – You will probably agree that posting and looking at pictures of animals, particularly young ones, is one of the joys of the online world. At least one study has found that looking at videos of cute baby animals, such as puppies, kittens and baby quokkas, was good for anxiety. So, feel free to do that.

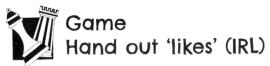

Game
Hand out 'likes' (IRL)

With a group of friends or classmates, take turns sharing positive messages or compliments about each other's strengths and good qualities and why you appreciate them. The goal is to create a positive atmosphere in your friendship group and appreciate your own contributions to it. Keep track of all the 'likes' shared and celebrate everyone's contributions.

Sleep

Loving yourself = sleeping more

Sleep makes up a third of your life. It underpins everything you do. Good sleep helps you grow, recover, do well at school and feel healthy and happy. And yet, lots of evidence shows that young people just aren't getting enough sleep. One of the culprits seems to be the presence of devices (phones, tablets, game consoles) in bedrooms overnight. Because of persuasive tech's tricks they are very difficult to disconnect from. If you sleep with a device in your room, you're more likely to be checking it late into the night, resulting in you getting a lot less sleep than you need.

How to get good sleep

1. Make sure your bedroom is sleep-friendly. Consider things like lighting, noise and temperature.

2. Remove all digital devices from your room. Or try putting them in the furthest corner from your bed so you'd need to get out of bed to check them. Set a time for putting them away every night.

3. Create a bedtime routine that helps you to relax. Include activities like reading a book or listening to calming music.

4. Design a symbol for a good night's sleep for your logbook. For one week, note how your nighttime habits affect your sleep.

5. In your log, reflect on the patterns you observe. Do you notice any differences in your other healthy habits on the days when you get a good night's sleep, compared to the days when you don't?

6. Based on your reflections, set a sleep goal for next month. Design your ideal bedtime habits that will ensure you get enough rest.

Scrolling and sleep

Although the blame for devices disturbing our sleep has been placed on the way that screens are designed (the invisible 'blue light' produced by screens interrupts our sleep hormones), sleep experts now think the bigger problem isn't the blue light radiating from devices but rather the 'brain alerting' effects of what we're doing on them.

If you're messaging on social media, checking notifications, watching videos or playing games, all these activities put your brain into a state of high alert, which is the opposite of the relaxed one it needs to be in to fall into a lovely deep sleep. The result is light and fitful sleep, so you wake up feeling grumpy and tired, and resentful of the need to get out of bed, instead of feeling rested, relaxed and ready for the new day.

If you think this is you, have a look at the sleep checklist on page 38 and see what you can do to improve things this month.

 ## Month checklist

1. Make a list of your strengths and good qualities. Build a healthy habit by recognising and noticing these more. ☐

2. Be mindful of your social media use and avoid comparing yourself to those you see online. ☐

3. Spread kindness by giving positive comments and compliments to others IRL. ☐

4. Identify what good sleep habits are and set yourself up to succeed with all your other habits. ☐

Month 2 logbook

Carry on your logbook this month by tracking your healthy habits from last month and adding in new symbols for whenever you notice your strengths and for when you get a good night's sleep.

Permission to Unplug
Month 3

Almost everything will work again if you unplug it for a few minutes... including you.

Anne Lamott

Thinking about happiness

What makes us happy?

From as far back as the time of the ancient Greek philosopher Aristotle, writers and thinkers have been pondering the question 'What makes us happy?'.

There are as many answers to the happiness question as there are people who have asked it. Some common themes do emerge though. We tend to be happiest when we have:

o **Strong relationships** – Meaningful, supportive relationships with family and friends.

o **Gratitude** – The ability to be grateful and appreciate what we have, and not compare ourselves to others.

o **Mindfulness** – When we can be present in the moment, aware of our thoughts and emotions, and savour our experiences.

o **Activity** – When we engage in regular physical activity which keeps us healthy and boosts our mood.

o **A passion** – When we find something we really enjoy doing, a hobby or activity that brings us joy and a sense of accomplishment.

o **Balance** – When we have a good balance throughout all the areas of our life.

- **Time in nature** – Spending time in nature and enjoying outdoor activities refreshes us both physically and mentally.

- **Good sleep** – When we have enough sound, restful sleep for our physical and mental health.

- **Opportunities to learn and grow** – When we have chances for personal and intellectual growth, to boost our self-esteem and confidence.

By thinking about all the little things that come together to make up the 'big picture' of happiness, you can start to see how you can build a happy and fulfilling life. Notice that none of the things mentioned in the list above involve buying things or having things. Remember too that many people have discovered that happiness is often found in very simple moments. You can make deliberate and intentional choices every day to nurture happiness for yourself. Some of those simple moments of happiness may occur when you make the decision to unplug.

Write down three things that make you happy here:

What makes me happy:
e.g. spending time with my dog

1

2

3

Finding balance

When considering the list of things that tend to make everyone happiest, how much do you think we need the internet or digital world to achieve happiness? Some of the items on the list may be things we can nurture using the internet, such as close strong friendships or opportunities to learn and grow. But some of the listed examples are things that you will only find offline, such as time in nature and good sleep.

What this seems to be telling us is that we need a balance between the online and offline world to fill up our lives with all the things that make us happy.

So, here's something to think about...

You don't *have* to be online

There is nothing compulsory about the digital world. It's there for you as a resource for entertainment, education and connection, but you don't have to use it – or at least not all of the time. You may enjoy using it very much and think that if only your parents or school would let you use it all the time, you would probably enjoy it even more. But it's only one option open to you when you choose how to spend your time. A danger is when you start to see it as the main, or only, option. If you do that you will start to miss out on all the other elements you need to make up a really happy life.

A closer look
Variety, the spice of life

There has been lots of research into what makes us feel happy and satisfied with our lives. One study suggests that the variety and diversity of our life experiences could play an important part. The researchers found that people who felt their lives were rich and rewarding had one thing in common: they enjoyed 'a variety of interesting and perspective-changing experiences'. This meant they weren't doing the same sort of thing over and over again but were choosing new and different ways to experience the world. It seems that having a diverse range of experiences, even if some of them might push us out of our comfort zones, can ultimately be very good for us, leaving us more curious and open to the world as a result.

Experiencing the world almost entirely through scrolling on a screen, however wide a range of content you are exploring, is ultimately only one type of experience. Getting out in the world, meeting people, experiencing things IRL, trying out new activities and travelling to new places all need to be a big part of your life in order for you to experience it as rich and fulfilling.

Is tech always the solution?

There can be a tendency to think that any problem (loneliness, boredom, etc.) can be solved by technology. There's even a word for this:

Techno-solutionism

This approach ignores the fact that many situations and problems are complex and varied, involving lots of different unpredictable elements – not least our messy human selves – and that some tech solutions may look right in the short-term but could have unforeseen long-term consequences.

If you choose to scroll through social media for hours, you may be stopping yourself feeling bored in the short-term, but are you missing out on other experiences (attending that daunting after-school club or participating in a sport with friends) that could end up making your life richer?

Messaging a friend to chat using your phone is an easy way to keep in touch, but are you missing out on deepening your friendship by having shared experiences in each other's company?

The problem with a lot of these choices is that you may not know the answer, or experience the consequences, for a few years or until much later in your life – for example, gradually falling out of touch with that friend you message online, but rarely see in person. Starting to think about possible long-term effects of the choices you're making now – for example, texting more and more rather than finding time to meet up with friends – is a good habit to get into.

Idea

With a group of friends, discuss the pros and cons of different forms of technology. What are the short-term benefits? Are there long-term advantages, or even disadvantages? What alternatives can you think of? Does the problem even need a tech solution? Here are four ideas to start you off with: **sleep trackers** (watches or gadgets that report on your sleep), **smart fridges** (fridges that monitor their own contents and automatically order food when it's low), **food delivery drones** and **virtual reality** (i.e the metaverse). Come up with your own too.

There are no black-and-white answers to any of this. There are plenty of arguments on either side, both for and against increasing the use of technology in our lives. The important thing is for you to think about this a bit more deeply for yourself and decide what you think is right. You may find yourself going backwards and forwards about this. And your answers may change, depending on the situation and circumstances. But try to keep asking yourself:

o   Is tech the best solution here?

o   Who, or what, might be impacted as a result
     of this choice?

Logbook prompt

Design a symbol for your own happiness, to indicate times when you feel really content, fulfilled and happy. Start trying to notice what makes *you* happy. Can you see a link with any of the healthy habits you decided to start tracking earlier on?

FOMO vs. JOMO

Earlier on you thought about deliberate and intentional choices you can make to increase your happiness. There are two approaches you can take when thinking about disconnecting from your devices for some of the time. You can focus on FOMO or you can focus on JOMO.

FOMO (Fear of missing out)

FOMO is the fear or anxiety that you might be missing out on something exciting or interesting happening elsewhere, and feeling that you should be constantly connected. It can make you feel restless, with an urge to pick up a device to connect again, so that you are 'in the know'.

What are some of the advantages or disadvantages of FOMO?

FOR

Awareness – FOMO could motivate you to keep updated on current events, trends, and social activities.

Motivation – The fear of missing out might motivate you to step out of your comfort zone and try new things.

AGAINST

Anxiety and stress – FOMO could lead to feelings of anxiety or stress.

Unfulfillment – Constantly thinking about what's going on elsewhere might leave you feeling unsatisfied or unfulfilled with what you're doing right now, and who you're with.

JOMO (Joy of missing out)

JOMO is the feeling of contentment and peace that comes from choosing to disconnect from the digital world and enjoy your present moment. It's a mindful experience. It's about appreciating what you're doing here and now, and who you are with – instead of worrying about what others might be doing.

What could some of the pros and cons of JOMO be?

AGAINST

Peer pressure – An emphasis on constant connection in your friendship group might make you feel out of touch with everyone else.

Missed opportunities – While embracing JOMO is positive, there's a chance you might miss out on experiences or connections.

FOR

Reduced stress – Actively choosing JOMO could promote a sense of calm and relaxation, as you're not constantly worrying about what you might be missing out on.

Improved relationships – Focusing on the people you're with and the experiences you're having could lead to more meaningful connections.

Can you see how some of the advantages of JOMO tie in directly with that list of what makes us happy?

Offline hero

Logan Lane, founder of 'The Luddite Club'. The club is a group of New York high school teens who meet every week to disconnect from their smartphones and take part in 'offline' activities together such as reading, sewing, painting and talking about books. The founder, 17-year-old Logan, says: 'I got a smartphone in sixth grade. So I was about 11. I remember being just so excited. My immediate impulse was to use it all the time. And so, I was always texting my 11-year-old friends and mindlessly scrolling.' But, during the pandemic and after she moved onto high school, she started to feel as though her phone and her relationship with social media wasn't healthy and had begun to control her life. She decided to give it up completely, to delete her social media accounts and to set up a club for people who felt like her. They're named after followers of a legendary eighteenth-century weaver, Ned Ludd, who was alleged to have smashed up mechanical weaving looms. The term 'Luddite' has now come to mean anyone who rejects new forms of technology (although the original Luddites themselves were not in fact anti-technology but were demonstrating about pay and conditions for workers). Not all of the New York Luddite Club members have given up their smartphones like Logan, but when they meet up they all disconnect from them completely.

Challenge
Digital detox day

With a group of friends, choose a day, or part of a day, to embark on a digital detox. This means no screens – no smartphones, tablets, computers or games consoles. Spend the day engaging in offline activities you enjoy, such as reading, drawing, cooking or just spending time hanging out. Reflect on how the day made you feel, any challenges you encountered, and the moments of joy that arose from unplugging.

....

Digital wellbeing is all about balance but it's also all about choice. It's your choice how connected or unplugged you choose to be. But giving yourself permission to unplug, and actively choosing to focus on JOMO while doing it, could help you find a balance between staying connected and appreciating the present moment. Embracing JOMO might allow you to explore what really matters to you and all the elements that make up a rich and happy life.

 # Month checklist

1. Consider all the things that contribute to a happy and rich life. ☐

2. Make your own 'happy list'. ☐

3. Think about the pros and cons of all the tech in your life. ☐

4. Try unplugging with a group of friends. ☐

5. Make a habit of noticing what makes you happy. ☐

6. Do more of it! ☐

Month 3 logbook

Carry on your logbook this month by adding in your new symbol for happiness and see if you start to notice the activities and habits that make you happy.

Don't be Fooled
Month 4

**Fool me once, shame on you;
fool me twice, shame on me.**

Old saying (with its roots in Homer's *Illiad*)

Uncovering the truth

Lies and more lies

Being able to tell what's true from what's false is an important life skill, but there are more pitfalls than there used to be, thanks to the internet. The digital world has provided us with a vast amount of information from all over the world, but it's also created more opportunities than ever before for people to create lies and partial truths, spreading so-called 'fake news' to a much bigger and wider audience. Last month we explored unplugging, but most of us will still spend some time using social media and the internet, so this month is about navigating this particularly challenging aspect of online life.

People have always told lies or spread information selectively, missing out important facts to manipulate others. That's nothing new and we can't blame the digital world for that. Some of the very many ways in which we can be deceived, hoodwinked, or fooled offline include:

o **Urban legends** – Word-of-mouth stories which are captivating and romantic. They seem believable (often we really *want* to believe them) but are either exaggerated or entirely false. These show you what happens when information is spread quickly, and emotion is involved (because it's exciting or outrageous).

- **Gossip or rumour** – In school, gossip and rumours spread quickly, leading to misunderstandings and false conclusions, often harming the people at the other end of the gossip. This highlights the consequences of believing and sharing information without verifying the truth.

- **Historical misconceptions** – Some historical events and figures have been described inaccurately or misunderstood due to biased accounts or a lack of reliable contemporary (modern-day) information. (The Luddites are a good example, see page 53.)

- **Advertising and marketing** – Advertising and marketing use persuasive techniques and selective information to influence us to buy something. In most countries, what they can say is regulated, so they can only claim facts that have been proven. But this is not true everywhere, so it's important to fact-check any claims being made.

- **Magical illusions** – In magic shows or card tricks, illusions, distractions and sleights of hand can create a false perception of what is really happening.

- **Detective and mystery stories** – These books are satisfying to read precisely because they contain 'red herrings' – misleading information and false clues – creating a puzzle that takes all our analytical skills to solve correctly. Reading them can help us to understand how false trails can be constructed, and how we can learn to pick them apart.

○ **Courtrooms and trials** – In court, often someone isn't telling the truth, or at least not all of the truth. Lawyers must present their arguments and evidence in such a way as to convince a judge or jury of the credibility of their client. This demonstrates the importance of how evidence is presented, and how it can be weighed up and evaluated.

'Fake news'

Against this background of offline deceptions, we now also have to deal with false and misleading information being spread online. 'Fake news' is a shorthand way of describing this, but it's quite a vague description of what we encounter and makes it sound trivial – which it isn't. Two more accurate words are:

Disinformation – False information spread **d**eliberately.
Misinformation – False information spread by **m**istake.

Deep fakes

A relatively new development in online deception, deep fakes are manipulated videos, images or audio recordings created using artificial intelligence (AI). These are incredibly realistic and convincing and can be used to create the illusions of speeches, conversations, or events involving celebrities, politicians, and other influential people that have never occurred. It used to be the case that we could always trust the evidence of our eyes and ears, but it seems we can no longer do that.

Idea

Grandparents are one of the age groups who struggle the most to correctly identify misinformation. They're also the most likely to pass it on. People tend to get more trusting when they get older, and they've missed out on all the education you've had about how the digital world works. The next time you see yours, why not spend some time sharing all you've learned? (If you have a 'Grandparent's Day' at school this would make a great activity.)

The tactics being used

With false and misleading information now having more speed and reach than ever before, and with convincing new methods springing up to produce it, being able to distinguish truth from lies is taking on more importance. Those creating fake news usually use a few common tactics that are worth looking out for:

○ **Evoking emotions** – Anything that makes you very angry or laugh out loud is more likely to be shared.

○ **Deflecting blame** – Attempting to blame other organisations or individuals for something they are not responsible for.

○ **Loading likes** – Artificially inflating 'likes' on a post to give the perception that a minority opinion is shared by thousands.

- **Creating conspiracies** – Conspiracy theories spread quickly because, like gossip, rumour and urban legends, people like believing outrageous stories.

- **Impersonating** – Pretending to be someone in authority (which is much easier to do now, see 'Deep fakes' on page 62).

A closer look
'Pre-bunking'

It turns out neither adults nor young people are very good at spotting 'fake news'. Ofcom, the UK government communications regulator, found that 70% of UK adults are confident they can spot misinformation – but only 20% could correctly identify it. And 75% of those aged 12 to 17 were confident they could identify it, but only 10% actually could.

Researchers at The University of Cambridge have invented an approach called 'pre-bunking', which may help all of us. The researchers found that giving people a taste of the tactics and techniques used to spread fake news on social media, through playing a game, increased their ability to identify misinformation in the future. In the game the players took on the role of a producer of fake news and learned the techniques used in producing misinformation.

The game used an 'inoculation theory', which is the idea that pre-emptively exposing people to the strategies used in the production of misinformation gives them 'immunity' when they encounter the real stuff (rather like how vaccines work). They found that after playing the game just once, people were 21% less likely to be deceived by fake news.

Ask yourself

You've probably already developed good critical-thinking skills, both in the classroom and outside it. Put those skills to work and ask yourself these useful questions when trying to work out what's true and what's false:

Who has produced this?
Be sceptical. Always question the sources of information you come across.

What is their motivation for producing it?
Who is this information from? Why are they sharing it? Do they have an agenda? Might they be biased?

Are they trying to manipulate me in any way?
Can you identify any familiar tactics being used here, like trying to evoke strong emotions? Are they hinting that there's a conspiracy?

What is the source of any facts mentioned?
Can I cross-check them?
Verify everything, especially before sharing. Always double-check news or information. Follow a variety of reliable news outlets to get a balanced perspective. Use fact-checking tools and familiarise yourself with fact-checking websites and apps to validate information.

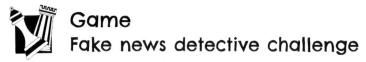

Game
Fake news detective challenge

Select some current headlines and stories from newspapers, magazines or the internet. Make up some fake headlines and stories that sound plausible. Design and print them out all in the same typeface and style, so as not to give anything away.

Gather a group of your friends. In the game they are presented with the headlines and stories and must work out if the news is true or fake. Create a points system, and the person with the most points by the end of the challenge becomes the Fake News Detective.

Taking your time

There's one missing element so far in gathering the skills together that can strengthen your ability to detect fake news, and that's TIME.

Scrolling at speed

Studies have shown that we are scrolling at faster and faster speeds through the online world than ever before. Back in 2004, adults averaged 150 seconds on any digital screen before switching to another one. By 2021 that had reduced to just 47 seconds. But pausing and taking our time increases our ability to detect fake news. Stopping for just five minutes to read more carefully and think can almost double your ability to tell fact from fiction. So – take your time.

Spreading fake news

There's a misconception that fake news is spread by those deliberately trying to cause problems. That may be the case for creating it, but spreading it is a bit different. Think back to those examples of rumours, gossip and urban legends. The people most likely to spread fake news are, unfortunately, all of us. Scrolling at speed means we don't stop and use our critical-thinking skills to work out if something is true and then, when we're doing everything online so fast, we often don't think through any harm we might cause in passing it on.

Logbook prompt

Design a symbol for your logbook for each time you spot false information, both online and off. For the rest of the month, record in your logbook when you notice it. And if you didn't pass it on, you could also use the symbol you've designed for recognising your strengths and good qualities.

Don't forget

Try to always report fake news if you identify it. If you encounter disinformation and misinformation online, report it to the platform and/or a trusted adult. If you encounter gossip or rumours offline, don't pass it on.

Offline hero

Finland (yes, the country!). The population of Finland was recently ranked Europe's most resistant to 'fake news'. Finnish people believe that no one is too young to start questioning the reliability of the information they encounter. Children and young people are taught from an early age to cross-check facts against at least three or four independent information sources and to question all online material critically. Their approach runs across all school subjects. For example, in art even young children learn how images can be manipulated, while in maths they study how statistics can be used to paint a false picture. The approach continues into secondary school, with students being taught how to produce their own 'fake news' to identify and expose the techniques used. The result is that the whole population ranks top in Europe for the ability to uncover disinformation and misinformation online. A big cheer for the Finns!

The S I F T Method

A simple technique pulls all this together and is as useful offline as it is on.

Stop – Take a pause whenever you encounter new information or news, especially any that stirs up strong emotions. Spend five minutes reading carefully what you have come across.

Investigate – Ask yourself the questions we looked at earlier about the source of the information, the author or producer, and their possible motivations and agendas.

Find – Look for an alternative verification of the story from trusted news outlets and fact-checking organisations. Don't click on any links (if online); go direct to your trusted source yourself and try and find the story independently.

Trace – Do your detective work. Trace the story right back to the source. Don't rely on rumour or third-party reporting. If you can't find evidence of the person or event featured, the story is probably untrue. Remember deep fakes though: seeing should not necessarily be believing.

 # Month checklist

1. Understand some of the common tactics used. ☐

2. Practise the questions you need to ask when investigating headlines and stories. ☐

3. Take time. Stop and think. Take five minutes to reflect on what you have read. ☐

4. Don't share any information unless you are absolutely sure it is true. ☐

5. Identify the skills you need to recognise misinformation and lies. ☐

Month 4 logbook

Carry on your logbook this month by tracking your healthy habits from last month. Add in your new symbol for noticing and identifying misinformation. Keep recording when you notice yourself displaying your unique strengths and qualities.

Healthy Relationships
Month 5

Kindness is a language
which the deaf can hear
and the blind can see.

Mark Twain

Making friends

Friends matter

We don't need hundreds of friends, we probably don't even need tens of friends, but we do need a few very good ones. Several studies have shown that the length of our lives and how healthy and happy we are throughout them is directly related to the quality of our close relationships with our friends.

Making and keeping friends can be harder in the digital age than it was for previous generations, so that makes it even more important to reflect on what being a good friend means, and how you can be one both online and off.

What makes a good friend?

You may not have thought much about what specific qualities make someone a good friend, beyond being likeable, but a handy way to start to think about this is illustrated using the word **C A R E S** (because that's what a good friend does).

 **Compassion** – A good friend shows empathy and cares about your feelings. A good friend is kind.

 **Acceptance** – A good friend accepts you for who you are, without judgment or criticism. They don't try to change you to fit in with them, or with their idea of who you should be. (This isn't the same as pointing out when they think you might be wrong about something...)

 **Reliability** – A reliable friend is there when you need them, they are dependable and trustworthy. You can lean on them when you need to.

 **Encouragement** – A good friend supports you when you're down or feeling low, and encourages you to achieve your goals and dreams.

 **Shared moments** – Friends create special memories with you by sharing experiences together and giving you their time.

Having good friends starts with *being* a good friend, so how many of these qualities do you think you have yourself? Look back at the list you made of your unique strengths and qualities on page 30. Can you see any of them reflected there? They may be called slightly different things.

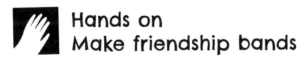 # Hands on
Make friendship bands

Gather together some pieces of different-coloured thread, string or wool. Assign each colour to a different quality you value in a friendship, such as trust, empathy, encouragement or kindness. Thinking of one friend in particular, braid, knot or weave the coloured yarns that represent their qualities as a friend to you into a wristband, tying tightly at the end. Give the band to your friend and explain what each yarn colour means and why they represent your unique friendship with them. Repeat for other friends to create a personalised gift for each of them.

Kindness

Kindness is the most important quality you should look for in your friendships, and a quality you should focus on developing in yourself. It's easy to be kind when we are happy and content, when everything in our world is going well or when we are rested and fed and relaxed. It's a lot harder when we're tired, angry or hurt. But those are the times when it's even more important to try to be kind.

#BeKindOnline

This is a hashtag that trends regularly, urging all of us to be kind in the digital world. That's not because people suddenly become deliberately unkind when they use the internet. It's because communicating through screens can make it harder to see, feel and understand the implications of our words and actions. When someone is in the same room, you can easily see the impact your words have on them. It's what makes you bite your tongue sometimes and decide not to say something that may hurt someone else, even if you're angry.

Because we can't see the facial expressions of the person we're communicating with online or hear their voice, it's easier to forget that comments we make can hurt. Additionally, due to the speed with which we all scroll, message and comment, sometimes we can lose sight of the fact that we're still communicating with a real person.

Try to be as kind online as you are offline. And look for that quality above all others in your friends and relationships too.

Good communication

Good communication skills build healthy relationships. Being able to listen to and understand what another person is saying, and being able to communicate your own needs and wants clearly, aren't necessarily skills we are born with. They may take a bit of practice.

Listening

Being a 'good listener' is something many people strive to be. It may even be one of the qualities your friends say you have yourself (go back and check your list on page 30). It's an important skill for building strong friendships and relationships and it doesn't just involve opening your ears.

 ### Offline hero
Diana Chao, founder of 'Letters to Strangers'. At the age of 13, Diana, a first-generation Chinese-American immigrant, was diagnosed with bipolar disorder and survived a series of mental health challenges before finding a way to heal through writing. At 15, Chao founded Letters to

Strangers, a community of individuals promoting mental wellbeing through the old-fashioned art of letter writing. Members write letters to strangers, and receive letters from strangers, anonymously opening up about their own mental health struggles and finding support. They motivate and encourage each other through their words. Letters are physically exchanged between members at meet-ups and 'create heartfelt connections and foster empathy, one letter at a time'. Letters to Strangers has so far impacted 150,000 people on six continents and helps about 35,000 people a year.

The best type of listening is what's called 'active listening', which requires your full focus and attention to concentrate completely on what the other person is saying, and asking questions, if need be, to make sure you have fully understood. Active listening isn't about solving anything, or coming up with suggestions, it's about seeking to understand.

Solving?

Seeking to understand?

Try these four steps:

1. **Focus** - Give the person who is speaking your full attention. Put away your phone or any other digital distractions. Maintain eye contact (but not so much that it's uncomfortable). Face the person.

2. **Empathise** – Put yourself in the speaker's shoes. Try to understand their feelings, perspectives and emotions. You can say things like, '*I understand how that must have felt*' or '*I can see why you'd feel that way.*'

3. **Question** – If you don't fully understand, ask open-ended questions to get the speaker to open up. (These are questions that can't be answered with just a 'yes' or 'no'.) You could ask, '*Can you tell me a bit more about that?*' or '*What was going through your mind when that happened?*'

4. **Reflect** – Show that you've really listened by reflecting back what the speaker has said, even summarising it. This not only shows that you've listened but also makes it clear that you understood them correctly. You might say, '*So, if I understood, you're feeling...*' (say this in your own words so it doesn't feel awkward).

 ## Challenge
Active listening

Pair up with a friend or family member. Each person takes a turn to share a personal experience or feeling they've had recently. As the listener, your task is to practise active listening and respond with empathy. Put yourself in their shoes and try to understand how they are feeling. After each person has shared, switch roles. Reflect on how the experience of being listened to actively made you feel. Did it strengthen your connection with the other person?

You can't always be there for a friend exactly when they need you, so messaging can be very useful at those times. However, if you have a friend going through a difficult time, or who is not feeling themselves, try to get together with them face to face as soon as you can to listen properly and offer support.

A phone call or voicenote may also be a good alternative to messaging if you can't physically get together. Studies have shown that the human voice plays an important part in our relationships. We can hear tiny changes in emotion when we are only listening to someone's voice that are easy to miss when we're distracted by seeing their face too. So, try out this form of communication with friends and family and see if you notice anything different.

Communicating clearly

Good relationships aren't just about being able to listen. They also rely on you being able to clearly communicate yourself. When you tried out the active listening exercise you may have found that the other person didn't always understand what you meant, even when you thought you were being clear.

Clear communication happens when what the listener hears is exactly what you meant to say. It involves you being:

○ **Clear** – Express your thoughts clearly and concisely. Avoid using complicated or jumbled language that might confuse your listener.

○ **Focused** – Prioritise the main point you want to convey, and stick to it. Avoid bringing in lots of other issues which may overwhelm your listener.

○ **Calm** – If you're talking about something sensitive, keep calm. Staying calm prevents misunderstandings and conflicts. Choose a tone that matches the message you want to convey. Avoid sounding angry or dismissive.

○ **Respectful** – Use respectful and considerate language, avoiding offensive or hurtful words that could damage your relationship.

○ **Open** – After you've spoken, be open to hearing the listener's thoughts or questions. Communication is a two-way exchange.

Texting and tone

Communicating effectively on screen uses the same skills as communicating face to face but 'tone' can easily be misunderstood in text. One study found that when people expressed their political views through text-only communication, they were more likely to attract strong disagreement than when their voices could also be heard. You need to take special care when communicating via messaging and text that your tone and intention come across just as you want them to. This may mean reading through things twice before sending. It is always worth taking a bit of time.

A closer look
Hiding behind your phone

Some people use their phones to 'hide' behind when they are in social situations, possibly when they are feeling shy or uncomfortable – such as when they're attending a new activity club, or a party. You may have noticed people doing it, or you may have done it too. It's always a good idea to try to put your phone away when meeting other people.

As well as making it more likely that you will meet someone new, who could turn out to be a great friend, you might also be able to help someone else. If there's another person feeling awkward and out of place, seeing your head down on your phone might make them feel they can't talk to you. It's much less intimidating if they can see your face.

It's not just in groups where being on a phone can be a barrier to relationships. You've probably had the experience of being with someone one-to-one when you were trying to talk to them about something important and their eyes kept straying to their phone or, worse, they kept picking it up. A word has been coined for that – 'phubbing' (from snubbing someone by checking your phone when you're with them). Research in romantic relationships has found that if one partner feels their significant other is always distracted on their phone when they are with them, they feel more negatively about their relationship overall. It's not a big leap to see how this scenario could play out similarly in relationships with your friends and family too, if they feel 'phubbed'.

All relationships improve when we focus on them. Don't let any of your screens get in the way.

 Logbook prompt

If this is not already part of your visual key, create a symbol for time spent with friends offline, focusing on each other and not your phones. You could be talking, reading, playing sport, watching a film – any time when you're catching up with each other and not scrolling at the same time.

Handling disagreements

No matter how good your communication skills are and how close your friendships, there will be times when you disagree. How you handle those disagreements is an important part of having healthy relationships.

The online world is not the best place for sensitive or difficult conversations. If you are trying to resolve a conflict, or are having an argument or disagreement, always take your communication offline and do it face to face. If this is impossible (perhaps you are a long distance away from your friend), then try a video call or a voice call. Just don't try and resolve anything tricky via messaging or text, it will make everything much harder for both of you.

Handling disagreements and fall outs carefully will help you to keep the **P E A C E** in your relationships. Here's how:

Pause and reflect – Before reacting, take a moment to pause. Don't react impulsively in a way that might escalate any disagreement.

Express your view – Share your view calmly and respectfully. Use 'I' statements to communicate how you feel and what you think ('*I am upset that this has happened*' rather than '*You have messed this up*').

Actively listen – Give the other person a chance to express their thoughts. Listen actively (as you tried out earlier) and show that you value their perspective.

Communicate boundaries – Clearly define your boundaries (also known as limits or rules) and communicate them. Let the other person know what behaviours or actions are not acceptable to you, for example, '*I don't want you borrowing my books without asking*' or '*Reading my diary is not OK*'.

Empathy and understanding – Try to understand the other person's feelings and perspective. Show empathy even if you disagree with them. Acknowledge their emotions.

Month checklist

1. Reflect on the qualities that make you a good friend. ☐

2. Let your friends know what you appreciate about them. ☐

3. Listen actively when others are speaking; give them your attention. ☐

4. Practise communicating clearly and effectively, especially during disagreements. ☐

5. Prioritise face-to-face time with friends and loved ones without phones and other distractions, to build and keep strong relationships. ☐

Month 5 logbook

Carry on your logbook this month by tracking your healthy habits and when you notice your unique strengths. Add in your new symbol for spending quality time, offline, focusing on your friendships.

Use your Hands
Month 6

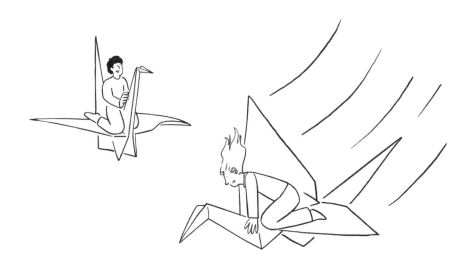

The hand is the tool of tools.

Aristotle

The world in your hands

The human hand is a pretty amazing thing. Your hands might feel unremarkable to you, but they're incredibly complex and versatile, made up of an intricate network of bones, muscles, tendons and nerves. They enable us to perform a wide range of movements from very precise and delicate finger actions to powerful grips. No other animal has hands quite like ours – they're built for both precision and strength.

Using our hands, rather than tools or tech solutions, can bring enormous mental health benefits and huge satisfaction. Using our hands for activities like drawing, crafting with yarn, trick shots, carving wood and even cooking, not only helps develop skills and increases mindfulness (one of the things we know makes us happier) but also connects us to a long tradition of human hand-created art and innovation.

If using your hands to create things isn't something you've done for a while, then this chapter is all about encouraging you to start. Perhaps it will inspire you to try something new, or even help you rediscover something you used to enjoy doing a while ago.

Quiz – What's your craft?

Answer each question by choosing the option that suits you best to discover which type of hands-on activity resonates most with your personality and preferences.

Questions

1. What do you enjoy doing in your free time?
   a) Solving puzzles or brain teasers
   b) Being creative or artistic
   c) Focusing on practical and useful stuff

2. What kind of new projects catch your interest?
   a) Building or designing challenges
   b) Creating something for others to enjoy
   c) Arty, crafty pastimes

3. How is your patience level?
   a) I can focus on a task if I see the point to it
   b) I can concentrate in short bursts
   c) I'm willing to put a bit of time into creating something special

Answers

1. What do you enjoy doing in your free time?
   a) Try: **Building, design and puzzle challenges**
   b) Try: **Creating beauty**
   c) Try: **Making something useful**

2. What kind of projects catch your interest?
   a) Try: **Building, design and puzzle challenges**
   b) Try: **Making something useful**
   c) Try: **Creating beauty**

3. What describes your patience level?
   a) Try: **Building, design and puzzle challenges**
   b) Try: **Creating beauty**
   c) Try: **Making something useful**

Hands on
Make something

Your quiz answers should give you an idea of where to start in finding a new activity you might enjoy. Have a go at selecting three activities from within the groups of suggestions below (select from just one group or from more, depending on your quiz results). If you want to know more about any of these art forms, research them online before you start. That's definitely a positive of the internet – it's a source of endless inspiration!

(Remember to check with whoever is in charge at home before you embark on some of these, especially building obstacle courses around the house, and using rice, powders and fruit for your art creations.)

Making something useful

These activities are not only fun to try but will also leave you with something useful and practical at the end.

Calligraphy
Discover calligraphy (decorative writing) with a calligraphy pen or marker, or even try out a Chinese style using a paintbrush. Experiment with different nibs, tips, brush sizes, ink consistencies and colours to create invitations for friends, signs for your room, or lettering for files and folders.

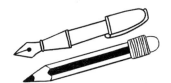

Cooking and baking

Choose a new recipe to try, whether it's a savoury dish for a main meal or a sweet creation as a treat. If this is your first foray into cooking and baking, keep it simple and choose something with a small number of ingredients, and seek help from an adult if using appliances such as blenders or when removing hot food from the oven. Follow your recipe carefully and enjoy the process of creating delicious food.

Crochet

Learn the basics of crochet to create a scarf, beanie or a small blanket. Start with simple patterns and gradually explore more complex designs. Plan your creation to be a birthday surprise for someone. Or you could design and wear something yourself that contains a message – perhaps creating awareness of a cause that's important to you. Try knitting as an alternative, or even hand sewing.

Fabric wrapping

Explore the Japanese traditions of *furoshiki* and *fukusa,* in which pieces of fabric and material are folded and tied, to wrap gifts and present special objects, rather than using paper. Learn the skill of making sustainable, reusable wrapping from cloth by trying out various fabric folding techniques. You could use this to wrap a special present for a friend.

Wood carving

Transform a piece of reclaimed wood into a wooden spoon, and become part of the long history of people crafting utensils by hand. As well as a spoon you could also try: a branch whistle, by carving a simple whistle from fallen branches (experiment with different sizes to create different sounds); or a wooden coaster, by crafting custom wooden shapes from reclaimed wood fragments.

Offline hero

Sara Trail is the founder of the Social Justice Sewing Academy (SJSA), in California in the USA, which teaches those in marginalised communities how sewing and textile art projects can be used for social change. Sarah was taught to sew by her mother and a teacher at a young age and wrote her first book 'Sew with Sara' at 13. Growing up she learned that her grandmother, who was enslaved, had made quilts, and Sarah discovered that quilts had a rich history in the USA of being used during the Civil War for secret messaging (if you displayed a particular quilt at your front door it meant that you were a 'safe house' for escaped enslaved people). Sarah set up her charity after she left university to show how the art of sewing could still be used today for social good. The SJSA runs workshops in schools, community centres and prisons across the country. Young artists involved in the Academy are now creating sewing art to explore social issues like anti-racism, gun control and gender discrimination.

Building, design and puzzle challenges

If you love a brain teaser, a puzzle or figuring out how things work, these activities are the ones for you.

Cityscapes

Construct a miniature cityscape using old cardboard boxes and other recycled materials. Build skyscrapers, houses, bridges and roads to create an urban scene – historic, present-day or futuristic. Be as creative as you want with the range and type of materials you use and the style of cityscape you create.

Domino chain reactions

Design and set up elaborate domino chain reactions to create satisfying results, or even domino art – creating pictures or words from the chain reaction. Experiment with varying heights and surfaces, or add obstacles to create challenges. Invite a friend round to witness the result.

Rube Goldberg machines

Design a Rube Goldberg machine – a home-made 'machine' that completes a simple task from a chain reaction made of everyday objects. For instance, one such machine might pop a slice of toast out of the toaster by sending a marble down an obstacle course to press the toaster's pop-up button. Use items around your home like dominoes, ramps, string, wire, weights or marbles to build your sequence of actions.

When you have been successful, challenge yourself to introduce even more steps into the process. You could adapt this approach to create trick shots too.

Puzzle boxes

Design and construct a puzzle box that requires a series of steps to unlock and reveal a hidden 'treasure'. This could be in wood, or you could even try to use some sturdy cardboard. Experiment with locks, levers and compartments to create a challenging puzzle for someone else to solve.

Wind-powered cars

Construct a wind-powered vehicle using everyday materials like cardboard, straws and paper cups. Explore aerodynamics and engineering as you design a car that can harness wind energy to move forward. Experiment with different designs to optimise the speed and efficiency of movement. You could create two and race them!

Creating beauty

If making art and creating a thing of beauty is up your street, try some of the following examples. Before you start, research in libraries or look online for inspiration and images from other artists working in the area, so you have an idea of their techniques and what you're aiming for.

Book sculpting

Turn old, unwanted books into stunning sculptures. Carefully fold and cut the pages, without removing them from the book, to create intricate three-dimensional patterns, shapes or even words. This is an unconventional activity which transforms discarded books into stunning art.

Fruit carving

Try out fruit carving and transform fruit and vegetables into decorative art. Learn different techniques to carve intricate patterns and shapes to create visually stunning displays. You could add your creations to your family's mealtimes for you all to enjoy as you experiment.

Origami

Explore the ancient art of origami by folding paper into intricate shapes and designs. Create traditional origami figures like cranes and lotus flowers, or explore contemporary styles to craft unique paper sculptures.

Rangoli design

Engage in the colourful Indian tradition of rangoli, a form of decorative art using coloured powders, rice or flower petals. Create intricate patterns and motifs on the ground at the entrance to your home, to celebrate special occasions.

Wire sculpture

Craft detailed wire sculptures to create three-dimensional portraits of people or animals, abstract designs or even words. Bend and shape wires to form expressive lines and shapes. Experiment with different gauges and colours of wire to add depth and texture to your creations.

Logbook prompt

Design a symbol for your log that represents time spent making something, or using your hands to create art. Try and log it at least three times this month, or more if you get inspired.

The journey and the destination

Once you have tried out a couple of these activities, reflect on how the experience has been for you. Remember that learning something new takes time. You may want to go back and repeat some of the activities to build on what you have learned so far. However – and this is important – though some of these activities have a 'result' at the end (a completed chain reaction, a crocheted beanie, etc.) the point of this is simply to find something you enjoy doing, and to enjoy the process as much as the result.

In life, you can choose to focus on the journey or the destination. In finding a hobby or an interest, the journey is the most important part. Getting fully absorbed in something you enjoy, which takes your full focus and concentration, is a mindful experience that will quieten the chatter of your brain and leave you feeling calmer and more content. No one else needs to see or be involved in any of these activities or hobbies unless you want to share them. And unless you decide to hone your skills in any of your new interests – for example, to enter competitions and win prizes (and that is brilliant if you do decide to do that) – your enjoyment is the only prize you need.

 ## Month checklist

1. Take the test and find out what new activities might be good for you to try. ☐

2. Challenge yourself to try three new things this month. ☐

3. Reflect on what you enjoyed, and what you learned. ☐

4. Do you want to carry on experimenting with any of them? ☐

Month 6 logbook

Carry on your logbook this month by tracking your healthy
habits and record each time you try out a hands-on activity.
How are you doing so far in your progress towards the goals
you set for yourself at the beginning of your journey?
Take some time to look back through your logbook
entries and reflect.

Go Analogue
Month 7

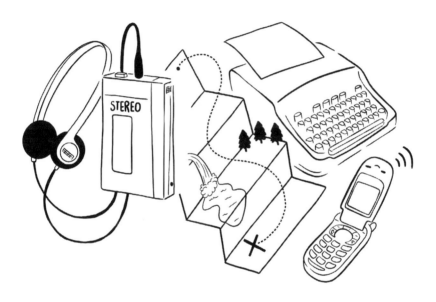

I'm team flip phone revolution.

Camila Cabello

Discovering analogue

Analogue technologies are old-school ways of doing things that use physical materials and movements instead of computers or screens. Think of them as traditional tools that you can touch, like vinyl records for music, paper maps for navigation, paint brushes and paints instead of software, or film cameras for taking pictures. These technologies work without using digital buttons or screens, and they can give us a feeling of nostalgia or being connected with the past.

Trying out analogue tools can be very rewarding. The experience isn't just about taking some time away from the digital world for a while (though it's a great way of doing that). Using analogue tools often requires more focus and concentration than their digital counterparts and so they can help make us more mindful, which is great for our digital wellbeing.

The perfection trap

Most digital tools emerged because they were seen as an improvement on their analogue counterparts. For example, typewriters produced results faster than handwriting, but then computers were much more versatile than typewriters. They promised to be more accurate and efficient, and to produce much better results. The appeal of digital tools in sound and vision came from the idea that they could deliver perfect sound and flawless images. So, although the move from analogue to digital was in lots of ways about helping us be more efficient, it was also about achieving 'perfection' as the end goal.

But there is beauty to be found in imperfection, as artists from Leonardo da Vinci to Jackson Pollock have always known. Things that are too 'perfect' can seem soulless, cold and sterile, and be lacking in personality.

As new digital tools began to take over and dominate music and the visual arts, artists, creators and the public began to think back wistfully to the authenticity, charm and warmth of analogue technologies. Vinyl records have crackles, and photography on film can result in unexpected effects when developed. People started to think that the so-called 'flaws' in analogue tools weren't defects, they were what had made them unique and what happens when human touch is involved. So, taking time to discover analogue technologies is about rediscovering all the joys of imperfection, about experiencing uniqueness, personality and the unexpectedly beautiful results you get when digital technologies aren't involved.

When so much of the digital world is about chasing unrealistic and unattainable ideas of 'perfection', going analogue for a while is a nice break from all of that.

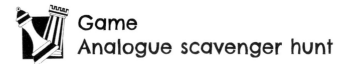 # Game
Analogue scavenger hunt

Materials needed:

- Paper, pens and markers

- Polaroid or instant camera.

Instructions: Prepare your list of analogue items to find, for example: vinyl record, old style 'gramophone' record player, cassette tape or player, rotary telephone, film camera, typewriter, old map, handwritten letter, newspaper clipping, sewing kit, basic mobile phone. Challenge yourself to find as many items from your list as you can within a specified time (for example, an afternoon, or you could even extend it over a weekend). You can explore your home, ask family members, or even visit local vintage or charity shops, if allowed. As you find each item, take a photo of it using your instant camera or do a drawing of it. After the time is up, enjoy looking through all your photos or sketches of all the objects you have found.

Exploring old tools

If you've been able to find some of these analogue items, have a go at trying them out. Here's a list to start you off. See how many you can think of to add yourself. These are great experiments to try out with a group of friends. You could even make them into a classroom activity if you are asked to plan or organise one.

Vinyl

Explore the world of vinyl records by listening to classic albums on a turntable. Did you notice a difference in sound quality? How did the experience of taking a record out of its sleeve and putting it on feel?

Typewriters

Experiment with a typewriter or a vintage keyboard to experience the tactile sensation of typing. Write a short story or a letter. Think about the effort involved in typing on a typewriter compared to on a computer keyboard. Does it influence how, or what, you write?

Internet-free mobiles

Use a basic mobile phone (one that doesn't have internet access) for a day. Reflect on the differences between communication in the past and now. Are some of the features easier to use or harder?

Instant or film cameras

Get hands-on with an instant or film camera and take photos in your house, garden or immediate surroundings. What does the anticipation of waiting for photos to develop feel like? Is the experience different to photographing on your phone?

Cassettes

Dust off an old audio cassette player and listen to music or an audiobook on a cassette. Explore how rewinding and fast-forwarding work.

VHS

Watch a film or TV programme on a classic VHS player or, if relatives have any, watch some old family 8mm film. Compare the experience to digital streaming.

Paper maps

Find a paper map for your neighbourhood and go for a walk with a friend or family member using only the map to navigate. How different is it to using GPS or mapping on a phone or device? Is going on a journey with a map different to planning a route on a device?

Logbook prompt

Design a symbol for an analogue activity or technology you'd like to try this month. Keep track of how many times you try it.

A closer look
Analogue versus digital gaming

Chess began as an entirely analogue game. It originated from India in the sixth century and is now played all over the world, with the two players facing each other across a board. With the advent of the internet, digital or online chess also became hugely popular. The first internet chess club started in the 1990s, but there was also 'play-by-email' right back in the 1970s. Many analogue games now also have a digital or online version.

Which is better when it comes to gaming – analogue or digital? It all depends on how you are defining 'better'. One piece of research conducted during the Covid lockdowns found that world-class chess players made worse moves when playing online from home than when they physically faced their opponents over the board. It had the effect of lowering their world rankings by several places. It may be that these skilled players had developed sophisticated abilities to predict their opponents' moves by reading their body language and visual clues, which couldn't be done online. It may also be that real-world strategy, analysis, pattern recognition and decision-making use different parts of the brain to those used in a digital context.

Online gaming can be a lot of fun, and also useful and accessible when we can't find an opponent nearby to play IRL, but gaming can easily become another of those persuasive tech time drains and take up unhealthy amounts of time.

Keen gamers should practise actively self-regulating the amount of time they spend playing games online (refer back to the **S O S** process on page 22). And all of us might be wise to keep challenging our brains with real-world, in-person games too, if we want to develop and retain all of our brain's incredible capacities.

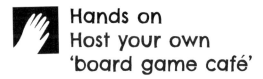

Hands on
Host your own
'board game café'

Gather any board games you can find at home, or hunt around in charity shops and ask your friends to find their favourites too, and set a date to host your 'board game café' experience. Set up a designated 'café' area in your room, garden or family area (if you have permission). You could even do this in a local park. Arrange the board games neatly, making sure you have a range of game types such as strategy, luck and cooperative games to cater to all tastes. Provide a brief description of each game to help the players choose. You could also offer a selection of drinks, including water, and maybe some finger food or snacks to recreate a café experience. Let everyone decide which board game to start with. After each game is completed, ask everyone to choose a new game to play. Continue for as long as your 'café' is open!

The power of touch

Analogue technologies all have one thing in common: they are physical, tangible objects that can be touched. It's worth thinking about what the action of touching and holding an object might give us. Reconnecting with our sense of touch through trying out analogue tools could help us experience an aspect of life that might be being neglected, as many activities such as listening to music, reading and taking photographs are increasingly taking place on digital devices.

Touch is one of our five senses. It connects us to the world in very specific ways. It's through touch that we perceive texture, temperature and pressure. From the smoothness of a polished pebble on a beach, to the gentle warmth of a hot chocolate, our sense of touch allows us to experience the world around us. When we shift to experiencing the world entirely through digital interactions, our sensory journey is reduced to the cold press of a screen or the click of a button.

Touch goes beyond mere physical sensation; it is deeply connected with our emotional wellbeing. A simple hug has the power to convey comfort, empathy and connection. When we hug someone, our bodies release oxytocin, a brain chemical often called the 'cuddle hormone'. This chemical creates feelings of trust and security, contributing to our mental and emotional health. A 20-second hug was found in research to significantly reduce stress and increase calmness in the person who received it (so count to 20 the next time you give someone a hug).

As you investigate all the different analogue tools you're exploring, focus on the specific sensations you get by touching them; the feeling of flipping through the pages of a physical book, the smooth coolness of a map as you unfold it, the grooves on a vinyl record as you run your fingertips across it. Enjoy the sensory journey.

Offline hero

Martine Postma is the founder of the Repair Café movement. Repair Cafés are community spaces, often pop-ups, where people bring along old household objects they have at home that need fixing. Volunteers who have repair knowledge come along too, to use their skills and fix the items brought in. The cafés are also spaces to learn from others about how to repair items which otherwise might be thrown away or become obsolete, when specialist repair skills don't get passed on to younger generations. Martine organised the very first Repair Café in Amsterdam in 2009, because she was feeling increasingly frustrated with the developed world's throwaway culture and wanted people to appreciate their old and damaged items and see them in a new light when they were fixed. There are now over 2,500 Repair Cafés worldwide – there might even be one near you. Martine is now involved in trying to change taxation laws in the European Union on new materials, to make repairing things more appealing than buying new ones.

 # Month checklist

1. Investigate a wide range of analogue technologies.

2. Discuss with friends what advantages and disadvantages each analogue technology has over its digital counterpart.

3. Focus on your sense of touch as you explore.

4. Hug someone!

Month 7 logbook

Carry on your logbook this month by adding in your new symbol for trying out a new type of analogue activity or technology.

Connect with Nature
Month 8

Nature itself is the best physician.

Hippocrates

Get outside

You've probably been told many times in your life to 'go outside'. It may even have annoyed you a bit. But we are discovering more and more about why being outside, particularly in green spaces, is important for our physical and mental health. Unfortunately, spending much too much time on our screens is one reason why we are outside much less than we should be.

Be nurtured by nature

Throughout history people have always seemed to sense that a walk outside in nature could make them feel better, think more clearly or even be more creative – without really knowing why. Albert Einstein walked an hour and a half every day to and from his office, developing his theories of quantum physics as he went. Naturalist Charles Darwin took three 45-minute walks outside every day. Composer Beethoven and writer Charles Dickens were both avid walkers, with Dickens habitually walking over 20 miles in a single outing.

We now know much more about why being outside can have such a powerful and positive impact on us, thanks to developments in biological and psychological research. Studies have shown that being in nature can reduce depression and anxiety, lower our blood pressure, make us feel less tired and even improve our memory and our self-esteem. It really does seem to be some kind of magical healer.

We don't even need to live in the countryside to benefit from the power of nature. Being in any green space (a park, a patch of grass, even walking along a tree-lined pavement) can have a powerful impact on our mood. Studies have shown that walking along a leafy street can exert a calming effect on people with ADHD, for example.

A closer look
Screensavers

Have you ever noticed how many screensavers and desktop wallpapers are images of nature and the natural world? And how many of them feature the colour green in their landscapes?

Science shows us that looking at the colour green, the colour of nature, has a specific effect on our eyes and our brains. Our eyes have specialised cells called 'cone cells' that help us see colours. Interestingly, our eyes are most sensitive to the colour green. This means that when we look at green surroundings, our eyes don't have to work as hard, so it's more restful. Green is also right in the middle of the colour spectrum, which makes it balanced and less straining for our eyes. This makes it a soothing colour to look at for extended periods. Blue is another colour that has been shown to be very calming for humans to look at, which is why we can feel so uplifted by looking at the sky on a sunny day.

One reason tech companies use the soothing colours of nature in wallpaper and screensavers is to keep us staring at our screens, instead of going outside. Don't let that happen.

Forest bathing

Being among or near trees seems to be particularly powerful for us humans (maybe that's why some people like hugging them so much).

In Japan there is an activity called *shinrin-yoku,* or 'forest bathing', which is considered by the Japanese to be a form of preventative medicine (a form of medicine that actually helps prevent disorders from negatively impacting our physical and mental health). It doesn't mean taking a bath in a forest; it just involves walking through one, and experiencing the sensations of being around, and under, trees. Japanese scientists believe that up to half of the benefits of being around trees come from the chemicals they produce called 'phytoncides', which they use to help ward off infections and insect invasions. They seem to work a bit like essential oils in aromatherapy. Even if we can't actively smell them, wandering among trees means we are inhaling them, and they have powerful positive effects on our brains.

Forest bathing started in Japan but is an increasingly popular activity all over the world thanks to its restorative effects. Charities and activists are now campaigning to re-introduce more trees into our cities and urban spaces, and stop them from being cut down, because we now know how powerful they can be for our health.

If you're feeling anxious or low, a walk in a wood or under the branches of some trees is a good thing to try.

Challenge
Try a mindful nature walk

Embark on a mindful nature walk by immersing yourself in the nature around you. As you walk, focus on all your senses. Listen to the rustling leaves. Breathe in the scents. Feel the air on your skin. Stop, bend down, and feel soil run through your fingers. Pick up leaves, stones and twigs along your way and feel the difference in the crisp, smooth or gnarly textures. Look at how the sunlight filters through trees around you (the Japanese have a word for this sunlight effect too, *komorebi*). Observe the details of plants and insects, noticing their colours and movements. Let any wandering thoughts come and go, and gently bring your attention back to the sights, sounds and sensations of your walk.

Grow something
Anyone can be a gardener

Connecting with nature isn't just about spending time exploring green spaces. Nurturing and growing plants can also reduce stress and anxiety, so gardening is a brilliant way to experience the power of nature too. If you can persuade someone to give you a corner of a garden, or even the tiniest piece of land, you can grow something. If you don't have access to an outside space, you can still cultivate your own piece of nature by trying out indoor gardening, on a balcony or a windowsill.

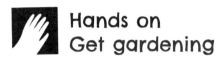 Hands on Get gardening

Select your plants – Begin by selecting the plants you want to grow. Consider the available space, indoors or outdoors. For outdoors, you could choose flowers, or vegetables like tomatoes or peppers. For indoors, herbs like basil, mint or chives are great options.

Prepare your space – If you're gardening outdoors, find a sunny spot and prepare the soil by loosening it with a gardening tool. For indoor gardening, ensure any pots have drainage holes to prevent waterlogging, with a dish or tray underneath to catch the water.

Planting seeds or seedlings – Follow the instructions on the seed packet or plant label for planting depth and spacing. Gently place the seeds or seedlings and top up the soil. Water them gently.

Nurturing plants – Water your plants regularly, keeping the soil moist but not waterlogged. Outdoor plants might need more water, especially in hot weather.

Gardening is a lesson in patience. For that reason, it's also a great mindfulness activity (see page 21). You'll find that some plants grow quickly, while others take time. The results can even vary from year to year with the same plant. However slow it is, it's always exciting to see the first shoots. And nothing beats the satisfaction of growing something yourself.

Offline hero

Ellen Miles, guerrilla gardener. Ellen started 'guerrilla gardening' in London just after lockdown in 2020, describing it as 'the practice of adding plants to your neighbourhood in any suitable spot you can find'. She had just started Nature is a Human Right, a campaign to get the United Nations to recognise access to healthy, green environments as a human right, but was looking for a way to make a more immediate impact in her local community. 'I wanted to find a way of making my neighbourhood greener,' she said. She admitted she had no idea what she was doing at the time; she'd never planted or dug or grown anything! But gathering ideas and help from more experienced gardeners in her local community, she assembled a group of volunteers every Sunday morning, and together they introduced nature into as many neglected urban spaces as they could find. Sometimes they tackled small projects such as scattering wildflower seeds on road verges, or planting bulbs at the foot of a street tree. Other projects were much bigger, like turning vacant land into community garden allotments. Ellen thinks anyone can become a guerrilla gardener and is an enthusiastic advocate of everyone trying to find small ways to make their neighbourhoods greener.

Looking after your eyes

The magic of daylight

You may not wear glasses or have any problems at all with your eyes, but there's no reason why you shouldn't start thinking about what you can do to protect them. There's actually an intriguing connection between our eyesight and getting outside more.

It seems that too much time indoors, looking closely at a screen away from natural daylight and sunlight, is particularly bad for our developing eyesight when we are children and teens. A study in Ireland highlighted the link between screen use and short-sightedness, when they found short-sighted students used almost double the amount of mobile phone data daily (so were on their phones twice as much), compared to students who were not short-sighted.

Eye doctors have found that being outside, away from screens, can protect our eyesight as we grow up. In fact, the more time you spend outside in natural daylight as a child or teen, the less chance you have of developing myopia (short-sightedness) as you grow older. Daylight on your eyes can even slow the development of any existing short-sightedness you may have by up to 50%.

One study showed that the amount of time outside needed to reduce the risk of needing glasses was only 40 minutes a day. Other experts have said that up to three hours outside a day is the optimum time for the development of healthy eyes (quite easy to achieve if you include travel to school, playing sports, and breaks spent outside during the school day).

 Logbook prompt

Design a symbol for your logbook for each time you get outside in a green space. Make a conscious effort this month to notice how much time you typically spend outdoors, versus indoors. Look at the amount of time you spend in each, and think about what kind of balance makes you feel healthiest and happiest.

Blue light glasses and screen filters

Because of our old friend techno-solutionism (remember that from Month 3?), some companies have suggested that one treatment for our growing eyesight problems, caused by too much time peering at screens indoors, could be wearing 'blue light' glasses that block the light produced by digital devices. In fact, a recent review of 17 different studies worldwide has shown that they probably don't relieve or prevent eyestrain, despite their claims.

So, don't rely on tech solutions to a tech problem, like those blue-tinted filters, screen protectors or special glasses. The best thing to look after your eyes is right outside your front door and it's completely free – daylight!

Three ways to help your eyes

As well as getting plenty of daylight on your eyeballs daily, there are three other simple things you can do to protect your eyesight. You can remember these as Blink, Stare, Glare.

Blink – Eyeballs need to be kept moist and blinking produces the eye fluid for that. But for some reason automatic blinking happens less when we stare at a screen, so they get dry and irritated. Make a conscious effort to blink more when using devices. Pause every 30 minutes and deliberately blink ten times.

Stare – Every 20 minutes, look up and stare at something out of the window, at least six metres away for around 20 seconds. This helps your eyes to practise focusing on longer distances, not just close up at a screen.

Glare – Reflections and light glares on your screen aren't just annoying, they can strain your eyes, so make sure you always position your screen to avoid any glare.

 ## Month checklist

1. Work out the proportion of your time you spend outside and inside, on a typical day.

2. Experiment with spending more time outside, in green spaces. See if it impacts other healthy habits, or affects your mood.

3. Find some trees and have a go at 'forest bathing'.

4. Grow something!

5. Practise the Blink, Stare and Glare techniques to protect your eyes from screens.

Month 8 logbook

Carry on your logbook this month by continuing to track your healthy habits. Add in your new symbol for getting outside in nature.

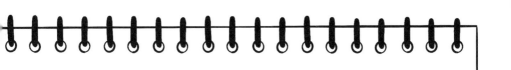

Build Resilience
Month 9

Fall down seven times
and stand up eight.

Japanese proverb

Understanding resilience

Resilience is the ability to bounce back from challenges and setbacks. It's the quality you need for handling life's ups and downs and it's something that will help you both offline and on – an important part of your digital wellbeing. Resilience comes partly from life's experiences; as you grow older you encounter more challenges and therefore more opportunities to practise it. But you can work on developing the qualities and mindset that will help you become more resilient even now. It's not some kind of magical superpower that only a few lucky people have. Anyone can build and nurture their resilience.

How to build it

Resilience has many elements that you can remember easily if you think of the word **T H R I V E.** People who have nurtured their resilience tend to thrive in their lives and get the most out of them.

**T**ACKLE CHALLENGES — **Tackle challenges** – Embrace challenges in life as opportunities to learn. Face setbacks with a positive attitude and look for solutions and lessons. Don't run away from any challenges you encounter. You need them to grow!

**H**EALTHY HABITS — **Healthy habits** – You've been logging yours in your logbook. They are important not just for

achieving your life goals, but also for building resilience. Practise looking after yourself through regular exercise, balanced nutrition, sufficient sleep, and hobbies or interests you enjoy.

Reach out – A good network of support to lean on in tough times is vital for building resilience. You need friends, family and other people you trust to rely on in life. Share your feelings and challenges as you encounter them. Ask for help and support when you need it.

Inner strength – Cultivate a belief in your ability to overcome your difficulties. Some of this may come from looking back at the evidence that you have done this before (perhaps in a different situation). Practise being supportive and compassionate towards yourself. Always talk to yourself as kindly as you would talk to a friend.

Value positivity – Focus on the positive aspects of any challenging situations you find yourself in. There is always a silver lining or an upside somewhere, though it may take some searching for. Practise being grateful for what you already have.

Emotional regulation – Develop healthy coping strategies to manage your emotions and handle bad days better. Engaging in mindful hobbies, or interests that develop mindfulness, can really help you to deal with any overwhelming emotions (see page 21).

A closer look
Doom scrolling

'Doom scrolling' is what happens when we endlessly scroll through negative news or distressing content online. Staying informed about what's going on in the world is important, but persuasive tech can result in us being shown negative news stories and upsetting content over and over again, making them hard to escape from.

Excessive doom scrolling takes a toll on our mental health. Studies have shown that elevated exposure to coverage of traumatic events, such as terrorist attacks or natural disasters, can lead to symptoms of anxiety, depression and helplessness, even in those not directly involved or impacted by the events. It can also impact sleep and our ability to process and deal with information, affecting how we perform at school. When we spend too much time scrolling through bad news, it erodes our resilience, overwhelming our brains with negativity.

Logging off and reducing contact with distressing news is not about ignoring the world's pressing problems. But to build our own resilience we must keep a healthy balance between distressing and uplifting digital content, to nurture our wellbeing.

Challenges and (healthy) risks

One of the threads that runs through all the research and studies on resilience is about how we approach challenges and take risks. People who shy away from challenges miss out on opportunities to face up to them, however uncomfortable they may be. Knowing you have successfully conquered a major challenge fills up your resilience tank like almost nothing else can.

On the other hand, challenging yourself and *not* succeeding *also* builds resilience. It can be an opportunity to learn – to understand what went wrong, and how you could improve next time around – allowing you to bounce back with confidence. 'Failure' can sometimes make you even more resilient than success.

It's hard to build a resilient life without taking on challenges and taking (healthy) risks. Healthy risks aren't those that put you in danger in any way, they simply push you a bit out of your comfort zone. Finding ways to challenge yourself and try new things that may feel risky will be important to building a resilient life as you grow older. This has been described as having a 'growth mindset'.

Challenge
Design your own escape room

Materials needed:

o Paper, pens and markers

o An object (such as a key) to 'escape' (optional)

o A timer.

Instructions: Gather a group of friends who will take turns designing and solving an escape room (a room that needs a set of puzzles to be solved in order to escape from). Each participant takes a turn being the 'designer'. The designer's task is to hide an object (perhaps a key) and leave handwritten clues that will lead to finding the object and escaping the room. The clues can involve word puzzles, number problems and visual challenges, and they could also be themed (such as 'Wizard School', 'Journey to the Moon', 'Murder Mystery', etc.). Ensure that they're numbered in order and are challenging but solvable. The final clue should lead to finding the object that helps the players to 'escape' the room. The designer should set up the escape room in a designated area/room using the clues they've created. Once the escape room is set up, gather the group of friends to solve it. Set a timer to add an element of excitement and urgency. Rotate roles each time you play so that each person gets a chance to be the designer.

This escape room challenge isn't just a lot of fun, it also challenges your focus, concentration and perseverance to solve all the clues, so it's a great way to practise resilience, which is important for your digital wellbeing.

Growth mindset

A growth mindset is a particular way of thinking that helps you learn, improve and become better at things. Instead of thinking that your abilities are fixed, it's about believing that you can get better at anything and can change, if you put effort and practise into it. A growth mindset helps you see challenges as exciting opportunities to learn and grow. So, when you face something difficult or new, don't give up – keep trying, learning and getting better. It's having a positive attitude that helps you become more resilient and confident in yourself!

Think of a time you challenged yourself or took a risk to step out of your comfort zone and you succeeded. How did it make you feel? Make a note of it below.

e.g. When I tried out for the football team, I was nervous and anxious, but I was selected – it made me feel proud of myself.

Logbook prompt

Create a symbol for facing a challenge that you have taken on, or one that has presented itself to you. It can relate to any part of your life. Log the symbol every time you feel like you have made progress with it this month.

Role models

Something else that can help us build our resilience is having role models. Other people who have overcome their own setbacks in life, or have taken on challenges and succeeded, can inspire us. They can be people in our own community or family, someone famous, or anyone else we meet or come across. They can help us see that anything is possible, no matter how difficult our own challenges might be. At different times in your life, you may have different role models depending on what inspiration you need. Throughout this book there are some that you may like to find out more about, if you haven't already heard of them before.

Write down the names of three people who currently inspire you.

I am inspired by:

e.g. Greta Thunberg

e.g. My grandfather

e.g. Marcus Rashford

1

2

3

Offline hero

Will Perry, Paralympian swimmer. Will lives with achondroplasia, a form of dwarfism. He has spoken out about the ableist attitudes (attitudes which devalue and limit the potential of people with disabilities) he has faced that have shaped his life, from childhood to representing Britain in the 2020 Paralympic Games in Tokyo. He was verbally and physically abused at school: 'I was picked up, I was dropped, I ended up in hospitals having x-rays.' He had a happy childhood with a loving family but started to feel self-conscious in his early teens when some people pointed, laughed and took pictures of him in public. With the support and encouragement of his parents, siblings and friends he pursued his dream of being a swimmer and representing his country at the highest level. Will now says, 'I think it created a strong resilience inside me that I now use as an athlete. When you're an athlete you face many challenges: you face injuries, you face defeats. I believe [my experiences] really set me up for being the athlete I am today. I think I would be less successful than I have been without that period in time.' Will now campaigns to change attitudes to dwarfism and asks people to call out any ableist abuse they witness in public.

Resilience online

There's one type of challenge you may encounter that is very hard to adopt a growth mindset for, or to see as an opportunity to learn. That's when someone deliberately attacks you verbally online (it happens offline too, of course). It may seem particularly unfair and unkind and hard to deal with. That's because it is.

It can also be hard to share and talk about, especially with adults who may never have experienced anything like it themselves when they were growing up and who may say 'just ignore it' or 'it's only words', which may not feel very helpful.

Bullying, cyberbullying and trolling

Bullying is bullying whether it happens offline or online. It's an attack on you, designed to upset you and make you feel small. Don't let anyone ever tell you that hurtful words are 'a joke' or to 'lighten up'. If it feels like bullying to you, it is. The problem with online, or cyber, bullying is that it can be very hard to escape from. If you have access to your phone or device all day and all night, bullies can get to you at any time. That's extremely unhelpful for your mental health.

Trolling is when someone decides to target and attack you on social media, either publicly through comments or privately through direct messages. It's the same as bullying, except that usually you don't know the person. You can waste a lot of time trying to work out why a troll has targeted you, but you should stop doing that. Trolls are motivated by lots of different things, but the important thing to remember is, it's not your fault. Trolls' behaviour reflects only on them, it has nothing to do with you as a person.

Staying safe

You need a slightly different strategy to deal with cyberbullying and trolling than you do for other challenges you'll encounter in life, but it does use most of the same skills and approaches.

Operating a zero-tolerance strategy can be hard, but that's just what you need to do. It can be harder for cyberbullying than trolling because it probably involves someone you know offline, and you may still have to encounter that person in your daily life. The following five steps will help.

**Ignore** – Try very hard not to respond to any unpleasant messages or comments. Ignore them. This is easier if you delete them (see below). Think of bullying like a fire that needs oxygen to keep burning; don't fan the flames.

**Delete** – Delete any messages as soon as you can (but see 'Report' below). Remove yourself from the environment, log off from the app, and put down the device. Don't read distressing messages over and over again, they will only hurt you.

**Tell** – Tell someone. It doesn't have to be an adult or parent, but don't keep it to yourself. Tell a close friend or someone else in your support network. Share what is happening to you. Ask them to just keep it between the two of you if that's what you want.

**Block** – Use any blocking and muting features (these are different for each app and software, so investigate) to remove access to your accounts from anyone who is persistently upsetting you. You don't have to explain yourself. Do what you need to do to keep yourself safe.

**Report** – For serious threats to your safety and mental health, report to the app or to a trusted adult. You may need to screenshot or keep upsetting messages. Ask a friend or someone you trust to keep them for you, so you don't have to read them again.

Cyberbullying and trolling, if you come across it, will test the resilience you have built up – but you can get through it with the help of your support network. Spending less time online for a while, so bullies can't get to you, and focusing on other things you enjoy doing, or being with your friends, will help.

Month checklist

1. Reflect on the qualities that help you build resilience, to cultivate a positive attitude to life's challenges. ☐

2. Put time into building your support network and practise asking for help. ☐

3. Remind yourself of times when you have overcome challenges and succeeded. ☐

4. Keep an eye out for doom scrolling. Log off when distressing news is overwhelming. Focus on positive offline actions instead. ☐

5. Stay safe online. Block and report any cyberbullying or trolling. ☐

Month 9 logbook

Carry on your logbook this month by tracking your healthy
habits and add in your new symbol for facing a challenge.

Make a Difference
Month 10

If you think you are too small to make a difference, try sleeping with a mosquito.

Dalai Lama XIV

Being a force for good

Everyone can make a difference to the world and you're never too young to start. Standing up for something you believe in, and taking action to bring positive change to your community or to the world is like being a superhero for a cause you deeply care about. It's about taking steps to make the world better, fairer and kinder. Imagine if everyone just sat back and didn't speak up about things that matter. Nothing would ever change.

You don't need to be an adult, or be famous, to make a difference. Plenty of young teens have made the world sit up and take notice of a cause they care passionately about. Greta Thunberg started her environmental campaigning when she was at school, and it has now grown into a global movement.

Stand up for what you believe in

It's simpler than you might think to start being a force for good.

1. **Find your passion** – Start by thinking about what makes you feel fired up. Is it protecting the environment, helping animals or supporting people in communities less fortunate than your own? Campaigning for change is strongest when it comes from the heart. Find something you *really* care about.

2. **Speak up** – Use your voice to spread awareness. You can talk to your friends and family, make leaflets and badges, even sew something (page 96) to raise the profile of your cause. For example, if you're passionate about recycling, share tips on how to do it properly.

3. **Small acts, big impact** – Bringing about change in the world isn't only about big protests, global campaigns, huge rallies or marches. Small acts matter too. Sometimes they can have even more impact. Help clean up your local park, volunteer at a home for the elderly or collect bottles and cans lying around the streets to take to your local recycling point.

4. **Team up** – Join groups or clubs that focus on the causes you care about. When you're part of a team, you can achieve even more.

5. **Write and create** – Express yourself and what you care about through writing, art or music. Write a letter to your local newspaper about something important. Create art, such as a sculpture, a t-shirt design or a song that spreads a message.

6. **Lead by example** – Show others how easy it is to make positive changes. If you start using reusable water bottles, or collecting bath or shower water to water the garden, your friends might follow suit.

7. **Support others** – Even if you can't directly do something for your cause, support those who are making a difference (see 'Being an ally' on page 159). Cheering on others who are campaigning and showing you care too can be just as impactful.

Remember, making a change isn't about huge campaigns or making things happen all at once. It's about taking steps, big or small, to create a better world. You're never too young to be a force for good.

 ## Logbook prompt

Design a symbol for your log that represents a cause you care about (or more than one symbol if there are several causes). Log every time you show your support, raise your voice or take a step towards helping your cause, or causes, this month.

Making a difference online

Social media and the online world can be incredibly helpful in raising awareness of a campaign or issue. The #OceanCleanUp and #AustraliaFires hashtags both reached global audiences online, raising awareness and galvanising support. The internet has the potential to help you reach many more people than you could reach in your local community.

There are pros and cons of using social media. Yes, it can spread your message far and wide, but sometimes it can also encourage people to think that just sharing a post is enough to help. Your feed might also only show you views that agree with yours, without offering up alternative perspectives. It's worth thinking through the advantages and disadvantages, and working out what the best balance of offline and online activity is, before you start your campaigning.

Pros of going digital:

○ **Global reach** – Social media can reach a huge audience worldwide, spreading awareness and encouraging action.

○ **Ease** – It's free to post on your own accounts, making it easy to start.

○ **Speed** – Social media allows a fast response to urgent issues, generating support and resources quickly (for example, in times of natural disasters or emergencies).

Cons of going digital:

- ○ **Lack of depth** – Online engagement might lack the depth of offline interactions, making it hard to build strong connections with your supporters.

- ○ **Accessibility** – The internet doesn't reach everyone; older and poorer communities may not have access. There are also those with disabilities who may find it harder to engage online.

- ○ **'Clicktivism'** – Sometimes, online actions such as liking a post may make people feel like they're helping your campaign, rather than actually engaging or offering meaningful support.

A closer look 'Clicktivism'

'Clicktivism' is when people show support for a cause online without taking any corresponding action in the real world. They might click 'like' on a post, sign an online petition or share a photo, but they don't do anything more meaningful. Taking a simple online action makes people feel like they are supporters, but it doesn't necessarily lead to people showing up to help in the real world or donating enough money to help make meaningful change.

When nearly 300 schoolgirls were kidnapped by the militant group Boko Haram in Nigeria in 2014, the hashtag

#BringBackOurGirls went viral. It was retweeted millions of times, even by Michelle Obama, then First Lady of the United States. But the uncle of one of the girls criticised the lack of practical support for finding the girls, despite the vocal campaign online: 'There is a saying: "Actions speak louder than words." Leaders from around the world came out and said they would assist to bring the girls back, but now we hear nothing.' In May 2023, more than nine years after the original kidnapping, nearly 100 of the girls remained missing.

People have always paid lip service (said they will support, but done nothing) towards movements or causes, but the online world and social media has made it that much easier. Asking the organisers of any cause, movement or charity what actions would be most helpful for them is always the best approach.

# Challenge Change-maker

Get a group of friends involved in a campaign or cause you all care about. Your challenge is that all of the activities you plan must take place IRL and not online. Here are some instructions and two campaign ideas to start you off:

- ○ **Choose a cause** – Select a real-world issue you care about, such as the environment (see page 156) or cyberbullying (page 157).

- **Brainstorm solutions** – Gather friends and brainstorm creative solutions to address the issue. Think about your desired result. Is it raising money? Changing behaviour? Changing the law?

- **Pitch ideas** – Each participant presents their 'solution' to the group. Use visuals or act out the idea, to make it more inspiring.

- **Vote** – Everyone votes for their favourite idea (except their own). The solution with the most votes wins.

- **Get going** – Launch your campaign!

Idea 1: eco-corner

Organise a mini campaign around environmental action. Create leaflets, or flyers, about a specific environmental issue you're passionate about. Make sure to use recycled materials wherever you can. Spread awareness among friends, family and neighbours. This could be encouraging them to make small, eco-friendly changes in their lives, such as reducing plastic use, conserving water or using public transport more.

Steps:

1. Choose an environmental issue that matters to you.

2. Research facts and statistics about the issue to include in your materials.

3. Design posters, flyers, and stickers or badges with compelling visuals and information.

4. Set up a booth or 'eco-corner' in your street or school to showcase your campaign (get permission for the location).

5. Engage with people and explain the importance of taking action.

6. Provide tips and ideas for sustainable practices.

7. Encourage participants to pledge specific actions to support the cause.

Idea 2: block cyberbullying

Organise a peaceful rally or meeting to raise awareness about the problems of cyberbullying – for example, encouraging people to talk about it openly and share methods of dealing with it (you could use some of the information on page 144). Invite friends, family and community members to join you in the school playground, hall or a public space. If all of this feels daunting, your 'rally' could even be as simple as asking for a chat around the family meal table.

Steps:
1. Select the cause and create a clear slogan or message for your rally (for example, 'Block cyberbullying!').

2. Plan the location, date and time of the event.

3. Design signs and banners with impactful slogans.

4. Prepare a talk or presentation to share the importance of the cause, including facts and figures on the impact.

5. Spread the word through posters, word of mouth, school newsletters and social media.

6. Ensure the event is peaceful, respectful and adheres to all the rules and regulations of the location you host it in.

....

Offline hero

Amika George, founder of 'Free Periods' and campaigner against period poverty. At 17, Amika, whose grandparents moved to the UK from Kerala, India, in the 1970s, read a news article on the BBC website: 'Girls Too Poor to Buy Sanitary Products Missing School'. The article highlighted how many disadvantaged British girls missed out on education when they had their periods. She started her campaign, #FreePeriods, from her bedroom to persuade the government to provide free sanitary towels and tampons in schools. She organised protests, wrote articles and started a petition, which gained over 200,000 signatures. Amika did use social media for her campaign, but her focus was firmly on tangible, real-world results: getting free period products provided in schools.

Two years after Amika set up her period poverty movement, the UK government announced that period products would be provided free in secondary schools. She said, 'I started my campaign before I could even vote. I think that's a testament to the fact that, actually, you can achieve change.' Amika was awarded an MBE at the age of 21, the youngest person on the list to receive one.

....

Being an ally

We don't all want to be in the spotlight and set up a completely new movement or a campaign; the world could be quite chaotic if we did! But we can all make a difference by showing up and adding our support to causes we care about. Being an ally means standing up for what's right, even if it's not directly affecting you. You might not start a big campaign yourself, but your support for it could make a world of difference. Movements always need allies. Here's how you can be an ally for causes you care about:

o **Educate yourself** – Learn about the cause you want to support. Understand its history, challenges and why it matters. The more you know, the better you can help.

o **Listen and learn** – Listen to those directly affected by the issue. Their stories and experiences can help you understand better and show empathy. Ask those leading the campaign or movement to tell you the most effective way you can help.

o **Amplify** – Share materials, leaflets and flyers to amplify the messages of those behind the cause or campaign. Your reach might inspire others to learn more too.

By spreading their messages to the people who need to hear them, you're helping their voices be heard.

○ **Speak out** – If you see someone who is campaigning for a cause you care about, or is a member of a community you support, being treated unfairly – stand up for them. Be a friend who supports and defends them.

○ **Show up** – Even if you're not the one organising it, attending an event for a cause can add your support. It's your way of saying, 'I stand with you.'

○ **Donate and fundraise** – If you can, donate to organisations that are working on the cause. You can also organise small fundraisers, such as cake or book sales, to help raise money.

Keep growing your understanding of the issue. As you learn, you'll find even more ways to be a great ally. Being an ally for a cause is about showing kindness, respect and understanding. It's about standing alongside those who need support and making the world a better place, one act of kindness at a time. You don't need a superhero cape to be a hero for change!

Month checklist

1. Research causes and campaigns to find the issues you care about. ☐

2. Remember to focus your energies on meaningful change and don't fall into the clicktivism trap. ☐

3. Organise your own event or campaign if you feel inspired. ☐

4. Be an ally. ☐

5. Find out what you can do to help; see what those leading the campaign or movement suggest. ☐

Month 10 logbook

Carry on your logbook this month by tracking your healthy habits and add your symbol for contributing towards the cause (or causes) you care about.

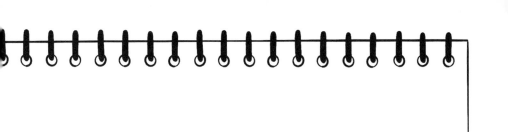

Awe!
Month 11

One cannot help but be in
awe when [one] contemplates
the mysteries of eternity,
of life, of the marvelous
structure of reality.

Albert Einstein

Embracing awe

Awe is that feeling of wonder and amazement you get when you experience something beautiful, grand or profound. It's what comes over you when you stare up at a coal-black sky full of dazzling stars, marvel at a majestic waterfall, stare up at the soaring ceiling of a vast building, or experience live music alongside hundreds of others.

It's not just a sense of wonder. Experiences that inspire awe leave you feeling small or insignificant in comparison to what you're witnessing – in a good way! There's a sense of respect that goes with it. When standing at the foot of a towering mountain range or witnessing a breath-taking sunset, awe reminds us of the vastness and beauty of the world and our place in it. It changes our perspective and opens our hearts and minds to appreciating just how extraordinary the world is.

When we feel **A W E** we:

Absorb the moment
Widen our perspective
Experience wonder

Awe is something that's hard to experience on a screen. The sense of feeling small but part of something greater than ourselves just can't be replicated staring at a small rectangle of glass. It's a uniquely offline experience.

The effects of awe

No one is sure why we have evolved as humans to experience awe, but studies have shown that it has powerful physical, mental and even social benefits for us.

Awe can give us physical sensations, like goosebumps up our arms or shivers down the back of our necks, a feeling of time standing still, and a slowing of our heart rate (making us feel calmer). It can also increase our feelings of connectedness to each other, lift our mood, and even make us a nicer person. In one study, people who had been standing staring at awe-inspiring eucalyptus trees were then more likely to offer to pick up something dropped nearby 'accidentally' by a stranger (who was actually one of the research team). The comparison group, who had been staring at a not-very-inspiring building instead, were much less likely to be helpful and didn't offer to pick up what the stranger had dropped.

It really does seem important for us to experience awe. Instead of spending all our time figuring out what makes us happy, we should also be working out how to experience awe more often.

An awe checklist

To work out how much you currently experience awe, read the statements on the following page and rate them on a scale of 1 to 7, according to how much you agree with them.

1	2	3	4	5	6	7

Strongly disagree ← — — — → Strongly agree

I often feel awe.

I see beauty all around me.

I feel wonder almost every day.

I often look for patterns in the objects around me.

I have lots of opportunities to see the beauty of nature.

Don't worry if your answers are mostly low numbers. The following pages contain lots of ways to add more awe into your life!

Hands on
Your personal moments of awe

Take time to note down moments of awe, and reflect on their impact. You could start by thinking back to times before you started this book, to moments that had that 'wow' impact for you. When you write about them, try to recall as many details as you can and use all five senses. See if you can conjure up the feeling of awe on the page and describe how it made you feel.

e.g. I felt awe when I saw all the stars in the sky while on holiday in the countryside.

Awe-inspiring experiences

Awe comes in different shapes and forms. Studies have found that nature, art and music are frequent awe elicitors, but we also know that something doesn't need to be physically large or magnificent to elicit awe. We can find awe in tiny, quiet moments too – think of the awe in watching a spider build an intricate web. Scientists think there are five different types of awe and that we all experience at least some of them. They also say that anyone can experience awe, and things like money or how 'successful' you are don't influence how much of it you can feel.

1. **Ability-based awe** – When we marvel at someone's accomplishments and achievements, for example, a talented musician or an amazing athlete.

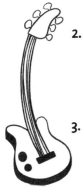

2. **Beauty-based awe** – When we witness something beautiful in nature or see an incredible work of art – standing at the edge of the Grand Canyon perhaps, or looking at a painting by Monet.

3. **Collective-experience awe** – When we go to a concert or a live event and experience the electrifying sensation of everyone feeling the same emotion at exactly the same time.

4. **Threat-based awe** – When we feel a touch of fear, such as when we witness towering ocean waves or an enormous electrical thunderstorm.

5. **Virtue-based awe** – When we are touched by hearing about incredible feats of courage and bravery – a soldier in war risking their own life to rescue others perhaps, or a stranger who has saved someone from drowning without a thought to their own safety.

Logbook prompt

Design a symbol for experiencing awe (or a collection of symbols for *all* the different types of awe, if you're feeling brave!). Look back at the end of the month and notice how many times you experienced awe. Don't worry if it doesn't happen often, or at all, just keep yourself open to the possibility of encountering awe.

Six steps to awe

Set yourself a challenge to explore awe and to be open to seeking it out in your daily life. Research suggests that, on average, people experience awe twice a week, and they're not all staring at sunsets or standing in eucalyptus forests! This suggests that opportunities for awe are all around us, if we look for them. Try these steps:

1. **Linger** – Don't be in a rush to experience everything – a journey, a walk, a visit anywhere. Linger, slow down and take your time.

2. **Unplug** – Put away your phone when out in nature, travelling, visiting museums or galleries, or looking at art.

3. **Admire someone skilful** – Observe someone who is the very best at what they do; an athlete, a craftsman, an artist. Watch them and marvel at their skill.

4. **Take an 'awe walk'** – Go for a walk in nature looking for opportunities to marvel at it. Appreciate the big and the small things.

5. **Use your senses** – Take note of all your senses; smell the air, touch your surroundings, lift your head and look around you.

6. **Move with others** – Be part of a collective experience; go to a concert, sing in a choir, take part in a group dance.

A closer look
The big picture

When we're told to look at the 'big picture', we're being encouraged to step back from focusing on tiny details, little annoyances and petty irritations, to try to make sense of something by considering it in its wider context. Experiencing awe could be something that might help us do that better.

The sense of the vastness of the world that awe gives us, and the smallness of ourselves in relation to it – the 'small self' as it's been called – expands our view of the world. It may even help us be better at critical thinking and more resistant to weak arguments and false information.

People who report that they often experience awe also seem to be better at listening to other people's viewpoints. In one study, experiencing awe right before a critical thinking exercise made people less likely to be convinced by weak arguments, whereas those who had only experienced happiness or amusement just before were *more* likely to be convinced by weaker arguments. So awe could literally help to sharpen our brains.

Compare the sense of awe we feel when we witness the vastness of the world with the sense of how small the world can feel when it appears to reside in a phone screen in the palm of our hands. It's another reason to step away from our phones more often!

The inner voice

Awe may also have an important role to play in our mental health. It seems the experience of awe has a remarkable power to hush our 'inner critic' – that little voice inside our head that is always encouraging self-doubt and negativity.

Awe puts us 'in the moment'

When we encounter awe-inspiring moments, something magical happens. The awesomeness of the experience captures our attention fully, leaving absolutely no space to listen to an inner critic.

Awe shifts our focus from ourselves and what's inside us to the world *around* us. When we stand before an awe-inducing landscape, watch a breath-taking performance or marvel at the death-defying feats of someone valiant, our inner critic takes a back seat. The sheer magnitude of the experience commands our complete attention, banishing any self-critical thoughts. Experiencing awe reminds us that we're part of something much bigger than ourselves, and we're left with a sense of vastness and perspective.

So, awe has a valuable lesson for us. While our inner critic is a natural part of our minds – and most people have one – we don't have to let it control our thoughts and feelings. Awe shows us that there are moments when we can escape from self-doubt and shift our focus to what's around us.

 Offline hero

Billie Eilish, singer. In 2022, Billie became Glastonbury Festival's youngest ever solo headline act when she stepped out on the Pyramid stage, at the age of 20. From her hit single 'Ocean Eyes' at the age of just 13, to winning an Oscar for her original Bond theme tune 'No Time to Die', to being not only the youngest person, but also the second ever person and the first female artist, to win in the four main Grammy categories, Billie inspires awe for everything she has achieved at such a young age.

Although she is active on social media, she uses her platforms to encourage her followers to use technology for environmental activism and other causes. She has completely deleted social media from her phone for periods of time to escape its pressures, saying that the internet makes people 'gullible' – herself included. 'Anything I read on the internet, I believe,' she said. She's also talked about the pitfalls of posting things online when very young that may not reflect your views later on: 'I said so many things then that I totally don't agree with now or think the opposite thing. The weirdest thing is how nothing ever goes away once it's on the internet.'

Billie plays live concerts to audiences of hundreds of thousands of people, creating her own moments of awe for those watching her.

Month checklist

1. Record moments of awe and reflect on their impact. ☐

2. Remember that awe can be found in small things. ☐

3. Explore the different types of awe, especially any you may not have experienced so far. How can you add them to your life? ☐

4. Practise silencing your inner critic by focusing outwards while you look for awe in the world. ☐

Month 11 logbook

Carry on your logbook this month by adding in your new
symbol for experiencing awe!

Reflection and Celebration
Month 12

A journey of a thousand miles begins with a single step.

Laozi, ancient Chinese philosopher

Reflecting on your journey

This is the most important part of your journey: the part where you reflect on how far you've come!

In life we can spend a lot of time looking forwards, setting goals, framing ambitions, making plans. But it's important to look backwards from time to time too. Looking back reminds you that you've achieved a lot already. It can motivate you if you're lagging, but it can also be a brilliant way of patting yourself on the back. Only by looking back can you get a sense of how far you've 'travelled'.

Acknowledge your progress

Look back at the goals and healthy habits you set for yourself at the beginning of the journey (see Month 1). Now flick through the book, focusing on all the logbook pages at the end of each month. Notice how your symbols have been logged. Look at the patterns they make. Some months will be busy, others a little sparse, but they all tell the story of your journey. Think back to those early sailors and their logbooks. Can you see where your own rough seas were, and which parts were smooth sailing?

B R E A T H E

Take a breath and think about your journey.

Balance – Did you strike a healthy balance between your online and offline activities?

Reflect – Have you reflected on your digital choices and their impact? Have you become more mindful in your scrolling?

Engage – Did you engage in meaningful moments with friends, family and loved ones, both online and offline?

Appreciate – Did you appreciate your friendships and put time and effort into strengthening them?

Time – Did you manage your screen time effectively, making sure it aligned with the goals you had set yourself?

Healthy habits – Did you practise all your healthy habits? Did you add any new ones along the way?

Evaluate – Can you now evaluate everything you have learned? What was fun? What was challenging? What do you want to do more of? Were there any surprises? What would you do differently?

Your reflections

Take time to jot down some notes here on what you have learned during your journey.

e.g. I have learned that getting outside for a walk always improves my mood.

Celebrating you

When you've finished reflecting, it's time to celebrate! Congratulate yourself on everything you have achieved. Whether you realised it or not at the time, you have grown during this journey (you may even have grown physically!). You have learned some new things and you have practised new activities and approaches. Even those things that didn't appeal to you have taught you something about yourself.

Making mindful choices

All through this journey to digital wellbeing you have been practising mindfulness. You've learned that the decisions you make about using the digital world are more likely to be healthy if they are down to conscious, deliberate choices. Keep reminding yourself of the big picture of the goals you have set for yourself (refer to the vision board you made in Month 1). Check in with yourself regularly to see if what you are doing, online or off, is helping you to achieve those goals.

Balance

Of course, there are times when you just want to have fun and not think too much about your life goals. You should always try to look for balance between making the most of your unique talents and abilities, and fully enjoying life. A healthy life is a balanced one, as you have learned by working through this book. Persuasive tech (page 18) is designed to throw us off course and thwart all our efforts to be balanced about how we use it. But you have learned all about those tricks, and why it's important to foil them.

 ## Offline hero

YOU, (write your name here) _____ ,
voyager to digital wellbeing.

This month's offline hero is you!

....

You made a commitment to starting a journey to explore digital wellbeing and you have followed it through. Take a moment to write down everything you've achieved offline that you're proud of this year. You deserve it.

e.g. I am proud of myself for turning up and playing for my team every week.

An attitude of gratitude

There are lots of different ways you can celebrate and reward yourself when something has gone right, or when you've stuck at something and persevered. You can shout 'Yay!', hug someone you love or go off and do something special as a treat. But consciously practising gratitude is one of the best ways.

Gratitude is not just about saying 'thank you' for good things that have happened or 'well done' to yourself for your commitment – it's an approach and attitude to life that can reward you.

Science has shown that practising gratitude can literally rewire your brain for happiness. When you focus on the good things in your life, your brain releases the chemicals dopamine and serotonin, the 'happy hormones'. This means that by simply appreciating the positive moments, you're boosting your own happiness levels.

The impact of gratitude doesn't stop at the brain – it extends to your overall wellbeing. Studies have found that people who regularly practise gratitude tend to have improved mental health, sleep better and even experience lower levels of stress. By cultivating gratitude, you're giving yourself a toolkit for building resilience (remember that from Month 9?) in the face of life's challenges.

Here are three suggestions on how to start practising gratitude and celebrating what you've achieved at the same time:

1. **Start a gratitude journal** – Each day, write down something you're grateful for. It could be a big accomplishment or a small pleasure – from acing that exam, to a sunny day or a cuddle with your dog.

2. **Random acts of kindness** – Show your gratitude by doing something kind for someone else. It could be as simple as helping with chores or sending a nice message. For even more impact, do it anonymously without expecting any thanks or acknowledgment (like sweeping leaves from an elderly neighbour's front path).

3. **Three things** – Before you sleep, choose three things you're grateful for that day and say them out loud (or in your head, if you share a room). It helps you end the day on a high.

By building gratitude into your life, you're creating a habit of recognising and celebrating the good things. It doesn't mean that you ignore or diminish anything bad or worrying, but it helps you to focus a bit more on what it is going right, which in turn helps you to deal with everything else.

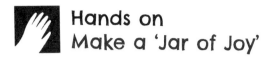

Hands on
Make a 'Jar of Joy'

Find a clear, glass jar and choose what you will fill it with (glass or shiny objects that will reflect the light are best, like marbles). Every time you have something to celebrate, put a marble in the jar. Put it on your bedroom windowsill, or somewhere where it catches the sunlight. Every time you see the colours it reflects, think of your celebrations!

Next steps

As you turn the final page of this book, you're not only ending a chapter, you're also opening a door to a new world of possibilities. The lessons you've learned and the habits you've developed are the foundation for a brighter, more mindful future.

So, what's next?

o   **Keep setting S M A R T goals** – Check back to Month 1 (page 16) to remind yourself how. This structure helps to keep you focused and motivated.

- **Break it down** – Divide big goals into smaller steps. Keep dividing until they are bite-sized and manageable, until 'I will win gold at the Olympics' becomes 'I will practise my shots on goal every day'. This makes them feel less overwhelming and more achievable.

- **Visualise success** – Imagine yourself successfully achieving your goals. Positive visualisations of success will boost your motivation and confidence. Revisiting your vision board from Month 1 will help with this too.

- **Stay positive** – Cultivate a positive attitude. Focus on what you've already achieved and believe in your ability to succeed. Practise gratitude.

- **Track progress** – Monitor your progress regularly. Celebrate small wins along the way to keep yourself motivated. Fill your 'Jar of Joy'.

- **Learn from setbacks** – Don't be scared of setbacks; view them as opportunities to learn and grow. Remember, resilience builds as you overcome more and more challenges.

- **Seek support** – Ask for help from your support network of friends, family and trusted adults. Everything is easier when we do it with the support of those who love and care for us.

Remember, your journey to digital wellbeing isn't over! In starting to think about what's next, you're setting yourself up to navigate the online world with knowledge, purpose and resilience. The next steps you take are the stepping stones to an exciting and fulfilling life – both online and off.

 # Month checklist

1. Reflect on your experiences over the last year as you've worked through this book. ☐

2. Celebrate your achievements and how far you have come! ☐

3. Practise gratitude, finding the way that works for you. ☐

4. Start thinking about the next steps on your journey. ☐

5. Keep your logbook somewhere safe, to refer to when you need it. Continue to keep a logbook in a journal or notebook so you can build on what you've achieved. ☐

Month 12 logbook

You're finishing your logbook for the year! Use this page for your final logbook entry, then look back on your progress and celebrate all you have achieved. The entries in your logbook will always be something you can read and reflect on. Keep it safe.

About the author

Tanya Goodin is an author, podcaster, public speaker, and founder of the digital wellbeing movement 'Time To Log Off'. As well as *The Teenage Guide to Digital Wellbeing*, she is the author of *My Brain Has Too Many Tabs Open*, *Off* and *Stop Staring at Screens*.

Tanya is passionate about introducing the concept of digital wellbeing to children and inspiring them to forge healthier, happier relationships with their digital devices. She has spoken in schools to students and parents for over a decade.

To find out more about Tanya's work, visit her online at:
tanyagoodin.com
itstimetologoff.com